Moral Problems

What Does a Christian Do?

Moral Problems

Michael Pennock

Ave Maria Press • Notre Dame, Ind. 46556

First printing, April, 1979
Fifth printing, July, 1984
145,000 copies in print

Acknowledgments:
Scripture texts used in this work are taken from the *New American Bible,*
copyright © 1970 by the Confraternity of Christian Doctrine, Washington,
D.C., and are used by permission of the copyright owner. All rights reserved.

All quotes of Vatican II documents are taken from *The Documents of
Vatican II,* Walter M. Abbott, S.J. (New York: America Press, 1966).

Nihil Obstat:
    Rev. Paul J. Hritz
    Censor Deputatus

Imprimatur:
    Most Rev. James A. Hickey, S.T.D.
    Bishop of Cleveland

© 1979 by Ave Maria Press, Notre Dame, Indiana 46556

Library of Congress Catalog Card Number: 79-51015
International Standard Book Number: 0-87793-177-1

Photography:
    Armadillo Photos, 46; John David Arms, 115, 226; Molly Barrett,
    110; Paul Conklin,134, 196, 216; Don Connors, 26; Robert Escobedo,
    cover and 176; Freda Leinwand, 21, 124, 187; Jean-Claude Lejeune,
    138, 158, 166, 171; Robert Maust, 65; Notre Dame Printing and
    Publications Office, 17, 56; Michael Rider, 36; H. Armstrong Roberts,
    cover and 148; Bob Taylor, 8; Paul Tucker, 206;
    Jim Whitmer, cover, 88.

Manufactured in the United States of America.

I dedicate this book to the memory of Charles Kerr. Chuck died suddenly on the very day I started this book. He was one of my students and represents for me all the beautiful young people I have been privileged to teach, especially at St. Ignatius High School, Cleveland, Ohio. His smile and his spirit are now in the company of the Lord. His memory is deep in my heart as I know it is in his wonderful family, his parents, Jack and Norma, his three brothers, John, Paul and Dick—all former students of mine. May our Lord bless them all.

ACKNOWLEDGMENTS

Writing a book can be a lonely job, but I was never alone because I had the love, prayers and help of many friends. I would like to try to thank them here.

First, I wish to thank my family: my parents, Frank and Louise Pennock, for being my first and best teachers of morality; my caring wife and best friend, Carol; my beloved children, Scott, Jenny and Amy, for giving me the daily love and understanding to complete the job; and my brothers and sisters.

Next, I want to express my gratitude to my great editors at Ave Maria Press, Frank Cunningham and Gene Geissler. Their encouragement has meant everything to me. Also, Charlie Jones of Ave Maria is a special kind of man who has done a lot to make my writing exciting and enjoyable. They are a real Christian community.

My thanks also go to some tremendous friends and colleagues who critiqued my book and gave me many helpful ideas: Dr. Tony Iezzi, Ph.D., was my key reader and advisor. His work for life is an inspiration to me and to all who meet him. Jim Finley has given me his wise advice and undying friendship. Fr. Mark DiNardo and Fr. Paul Hritz keep encouraging me and helping me in my vocation as a religious educator. I owe very much to them, not only for the education they gave me but more importantly for the light of Jesus they show me. My high school friend, Jerry Bednar, Esq., lent his legal advice and keen mind to the manuscript. My colleague, Sr. Carolyn Capuano, H.M., kept my male point of view from being too unbalanced. My friend, Bert Polito, encouraged me every step of the way. I am very proud of Bert, a former student of mine who now teaches with me. My colleagues and friends at St. Ignatius High School are a great source of strength to me—especially Jim Skerl, Marty Dybicz, Sue Ann Riley, Larry Belt, S.J., Ron Torina, S.J., and Tom Ankenbrandt, S.J. I appreciate in a special way the continuing encouragement and help of my friend Dan Conway of Walsh Jesuit High School.

Jeanette Kramer deserves much credit for her excellent typing job on the final draft of the book.

My professors at Akron University where I am enrolled in a doctoral program deserve my thanks for their continuing encouragement, especially Dr. Fred Schultz, Dr. Larry Bradley, and Dr. Steve Thompson. I respect them very much and appreciate the valuable help they have given me in my professional career.

Last, I would like to express my deepest appreciation to my students, past and present, at St. Ignatius High School. I have been blessed over the years not only with outstanding students, but outstanding young men. Their attention in class and their response to my teaching have been great sources of joy. I am privileged to teach them. I love them all and thank the Lord for calling me to share his good news with them. The following young men deserve mention for offering their insights on this book: Bob Kleinhenz, Kev Grady, Steve Russell, Wally Milligan, Ken Golonka, Rog Mastroianni, Gerry Karp, Dan Dever, Denny Rehor, Ray Olle, Kev McGowan, Ray Vivolo, Ted Donnelly, Chris Joy, Dick Lawless, Mike Rees, Jim Graven, Fred DiSanto, Tom Fanta, Ken Fox, Dan Hurley, Chris Miller and Dave Zubricky.

To all of these and all others who have loved me I say thanks and God bless you.

Michael Pennock

Contents

1 Introduction: Getting Started 9

2 The "STOP" Sign 27

3 The STOP Sign, Continued 57

4 The STOP Sign, Concluded 89

5 The STOP Sign Applied 111

6 Moral Pluralism 139

7 Morality and Sin 159

8 Solving Moral Problems: What About Life? 177

9 Solving Moral Problems: Truth and Justice 197

10 Reasoning Morally and Conclusion 217

Quiz on Book 227

Answers to Quiz 239

1

Introduction: Getting Started

Foresight is to be sought, for hindsight is dearly bought.
—Robert Southwell, S.J.
English martyr

This book is about moral problems. Furthermore, it presents a method for solving moral problems. Certainly, it does not take a lot of imagination to notice that the world is plagued with problems. Many of these problems deal with morality. Some are easy to solve; others are very complex and take much thought and hard work to begin to arrive at a solution. Moral problems take many forms: some deal with personal morality; others are social problems; many are interpersonal and have various consequences. A quick glance at the following list will give you some idea of the wide variety of moral problems troubling contemporary men and women:

- male and female college students living together
- the arms race
- cloning
- abortion on demand
- price-fixing
- cheating on exams
- pollution of the environment
- abuse of drugs
- pornography
- poverty and prejudice
- vandalism
- euthanasia
- driving a car under the influence of alcohol

For Discussion:

Which of the above problems deal mainly with "personal" morality; which with "social" morality? Which would have to be listed in both categories? Explain your answers.

Very few people in our contemporary American society would deny that there are moral problems with which we have to deal almost on a daily basis. In fact, many people would hold that most, if not all, of the issues listed above are moral problems. But these people also have difficulty agreeing on a method for solving such moral problems. Ours is a pluralistic society with many philosophies, religions, systems of thought and ways of looking at reality. As a result, very few people can agree on one correct way to solve problems. This is why in the political arena there are Democrats, Republicans, Independents and Socialists. People have various starting points for attacking issues and problems.

At this beginning point of your study, it would be good for you to examine your own stance in solving moral issues and problems. The exercise below describes five major moral positions. Each position is a starting point for some people in our society. Mark your reaction to each position in the space provided: (1) means that you strongly agree with the position described; on the other extreme, (5) means that you very strongly disagree with the position as stated; the numbers in between represent shades of agreement or disagreement.

MORAL POSITIONS

1. You should act to your own best advantage—whatever brings you the greatest happiness. (For example, it is OK to lie if it is likely that things will be better for you.)

```
1    2    3    4    5
```

2. Given the particular situation, you should do whatever you think will lead to the greatest good for the greatest number of people. (For example, it is OK to steal if it will lead to things turning out well for most people involved.)

3. Certain moral principles have evolved over time because people have found that, if they are followed, life tends to be better for the majority of people. People should guide their lives by these principles irrespective of the particular situation in which they find themselves. (For example, abortion is always wrong.)

4. "Do unto others as you would have them do unto you." (For example, you should help out a person in trouble if, in a similar situation, you would want someone to do the same for you.)

5. The right way to act is to follow the majority of people in the society in which you live. (For example, if it is the custom of fellow classmates to cheat on a particularly difficult exam, then it is OK to cheat.)

For Discussion:

Which of these moral positions is the least Christian? the most Christian? Which position do you think most Americans follow?

Although each of the moral systems exemplified above will be referred to later in the book, you may wish to know something more about them now. Positions 1 and 2 are known as *teleological* or *consequentialist* positions. Teleological refers to the end or out-come of an action or, simply put, the consequences of the act. These positions hold that the measuring stick for morality is the consequence of the act, that is, whether more good than evil is produced by it. Position 1 is *egotist* because it is concerned with the greatest good that results for the individual; position 2 is some-times known as *utilitarian* because it says that the usefulness of an action is measured by the greatest good it does for the most people involved.

Those who study morality term position 3 *deontological.* Deontology is not as concerned with the consequences of an act as it is with whether a person has fulfilled his or her duty to obey specific moral laws. It represents a concern for duty or moral obligation; it is most concerned with what is binding.

Position 4 comes close to a saying of Jesus on how the Chris-tian should treat others. It sees morality as a *positive response* to the neighbor in need.

Position 5 is a *morality of conformity.* Rightness is judged by the majority of people who live in a particular society at a par-ticular time; wrongness is determined by the majority opinion, also.

THE PLAN OF THIS BOOK

What this book attempts to do is to present a *method* for solving moral problems. In addition, it will provide you with a number of moral problems to work through. It will try to show you some of the differences between Catholic moral decision-making and approaches used by others in our contemporary society. It will discuss the topic of sin and relate that concept to the notion of right and wrong. Much of the original inspiration for the method described here comes from the writings of Professor Daniel P. Maguire, a Catholic moralist from Marquette University. Many other theologians, and especially church teaching, have helped in formulating the method. In brief summary form—easy to memorize—the method looks like this:

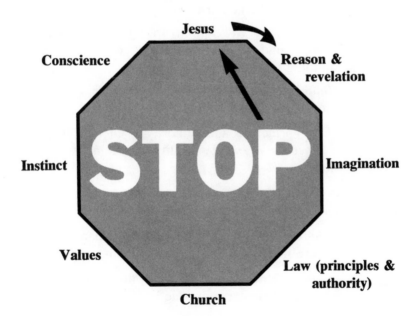

The STOP sign refers to four concepts which will be discussed in Chapter 2. They include the following:

> • SEARCH out the facts of the issue by asking key questions like what, why, who, where, when and how.

> • THINK about the alternatives to your proposed action and consider the consequences.

> • OTHERS should be consulted and the effect of the action on others should be considered.

> • PRAY to our Lord for guidance.

Chapter 3 will discuss the following elements around the STOP sign:

> *Jesus:* What does he have to say about how we should act? Is the action a loving and serving one?

> *Reason and Revelation:* In light of human intelligence and divine revelation, what is the human thing to do?

> *Imagination:* What role does creative insight have in solving moral problems?

> *Law* (principles and authority): Of what help is the *objective norm* of morality in making moral decisions?

Chapter 4 will treat the rest of the elements around the STOP sign.

> *Church:* What teachings of the Christian community are helpful in doing the right thing?

> *Values:* How should I rank the values involved in a particular moral action?

> *Instinct:* What help can one's "moral sensibility" be in the solution of moral problems?

> *Conscience:* What role does conscience, the *subjective norm* of morality, play in moral decision-making?

The rest of the book, then, treats the following topics:

Chapter 5 applies the STOP sign method to the moral issue of premarital sex.

Chapter 6 discusses the theme of moral pluralism, using the topic of abortion as a typical controversial issue on which there is little agreement in contemporary society.

Chapter 7 treats the topic of sin.

Chapters 8, 9 and 10 deal with specific moral issues and give a number of cases for the reader to reflect on and apply what has been learned in the book. The topics in these chapters include life issues, issues of truth, justice and moral reasoning.

SOME DEFINITIONS

At best, terms like "morality," "ethics," "Christian morality," "Catholic morality" and "the new morality" can make any discussion about moral problems confusing. Without getting into an extensive debate over the fine differences among these terms, this section will offer three definitions of "morality" which seem essential before further discussion of the method treated in this book. By way of introduction, though, we might comment that morality has to do with the rightness and wrongness of actions and attitudes.

Before offering any further definition, you may wish to look at certain actions/attitudes and judge whether they are right or wrong. Keep in mind that moral issues are rarely as clear-cut as this exercise might suggest. Put an *R* in the space provided if you think the statement is right; *W* if you think it is wrong; *D* if you honestly don't know if it is right or wrong.

Right and Wrong

—— 1. "Since Jesus said 'the poor will be with you always,' I don't see much reason for social welfare programs."

—— 2. "If the teacher is unfair to me, there is nothing wrong with cheating."

—— 3. "Premarital sex is all right if the two people love each other."

—— 4. "Abortion on demand is an unspeakable crime."

—— 5. "It doesn't make much difference if I curse (that is, take God's name in vain) as long as I don't really mean what I say."

—— 6. "Women should not really be competing for men's jobs."

—— 7. "Going to Mass just to please one's parents is wrong."

—— 8. "I would lie to protect a friend's reputation."

—— 9. "People are out to get you so you better watch out."

—— 10. "Life is the survival of the fittest."

—— 11. "Something is OK if you don't hurt anyone."

—— 12. "What is important is not that you have achieved your goals but that you have tried."

—— 13. "Teenage drinking in moderation is OK."

—— 14. "There are virtually no good reasons for breaking a law."

—— 15. "Talking about someone's faults is all right as long as the person does not find out."

—— 16. "Getting bombed is just the individual's business."

—— 17. "Not befriending a person because of his or her race is not that big an issue."

—— 18. "Eating junk food is my own business."

—— 19. "Smoking cigarettes and smoking 'joints' are the same thing."

—— 20. "Driving is a right—it is not a privilege."

For Discussion:

1. If you said that one of the statements above was wrong, what made it wrong?

2. Go through the list and look at your answers marked W. Did you consider them wrong because of the intention or the circumstances? Do you think some actions in and of themselves are so bad that they are always wrong? Explain.

What is morality?

Our first definition of morality comes from the German theologian Franz Bockle. He defines moral theology as that "part of theology that searches for the norms of free human conduct in the light of revelation."[1] There are two important elements in this definition of moral theology.

Morality is concerned with free human conduct. The big assumption in Bockle's definition of morality is that people can freely perform human acts. Morality presupposes freedom. It takes for granted that humans are not absolutely determined. Absolute determination means that either one's heredity or environment, or both, totally cause the person to act in a certain way. Theories of absolute determination claim that humans are not free—they only think they are. Karl Marx, for example, maintained that economics—money—is what ultimately makes people do what they do. He would say that the real underlying reason for education is to get a better job and make more money. All the other reasons are phony. Humans are not free. If Marx and other absolute determinists were correct there would be no morality, there would be no right or wrong. Freedom of choice is necessary to do good—or to do bad.

The Christian can admit that to a degree we are conditioned, we are determined. We did not choose our own set of parents, we did not choose to be born in the 20th century, in America, of a particular race. We did not choose our sex. We were born with

---

[1] *Fundamental Concepts of Moral Theology* (New York: Paulist Press, 1968), p. 1.

certain talents and certain limitations. But Christians—as we shall see in more detail in Chapter 4—hold that we are born with a certain degree of freedom. (For example, you can now choose to stop reading this book or to continue to do so.) Freedom means that we can make choices about our lives, about our actions. For the Christian, freedom also means that out of love he or she can decide for God. Morality concerns what we do with our freedom.

Unlike ethics, which searches for the norms of human conduct in light of reason alone, Christian morality is guided by revelation. Human intelligence can be a powerful guide in working out moral problems. However, the Christian believes that he or she has more than reason to help him or her. Christians believe that God revealed himself in human history. Supernatural revelation refers to God's freely chosen self-communication to humankind. We believe that God "unveiled" (the literal translation for "revelation") himself in human history by inviting people to share his very life, by addressing people as friends, by moving among them in order to receive them into his own company. The story of God's self-disclosure is known as salvation history. It is recorded in the Old Testament as the chronicle of Yahweh's dealings with the Jews. It is fulfilled in the New Testament when God's own Son, Jesus Christ, came as God's final Word, his total self-communication.

When joined to our Lord Jesus Christ, who is the perfect norm and guide to Christian moral response, we believe that reflection on and praying with the scriptures are powerful helps in solving moral problems. In revealing himself, especially in his son Jesus, Yahweh gave men and women an insight into what it means to be really alive, to be really human. In communicating his love, he showed us what our destiny is and gave us powerful guides in directing our lives to him. People who accept in faith God's revelation, especially life in Jesus our Lord, have much help in solving moral problems. (This fact will be discussed at length in the next few chapters.)

A second definition of morality

The second definition comes from the French theologian/philosopher Antonin Sertillanges: "Morality is the science of what man ought to be by reason of what he is."[2] This definition has three very important elements.

Morality is a science. By definition, science is an open-ended study of something. The task of science is never complete. It always seeks new answers; it continuously adds new information to the data already collected. So, too, morality is a science. The more we learn about ourselves, the more we learn about what is right and wrong. For example, Western civilization for hundreds of years tolerated slavery. Many sophisticated arguments were made trying to justify it. In our own country, it was only about 100 years ago that we found it irreconcilable with the dignity of the human person, with the equality we proclaim so boldly in the Constitution. The concept of equality we put into the constitutional amendments after the Civil War is finally being taken seriously today. Today, the quest for equality continues. Women's rights movements arguing for equal pay for equal work, for example, are sensitizing both citizens and lawmakers alike to the gross injustices which are committed, often unthinkingly, against women.

Because our knowledge of human conditions changes, morality can and does change. Another example is that for a period of time in the Middle Ages, the borrowing and lending of money at interest were considered seriously sinful. In a feudal economy, there were good reasons for condemning the charging of interest. As the economy moved to the villages and businesses changed, it made a lot of sense to lend money at interest. The economy had so changed that the morality of what was considered right and wrong in the use of money also changed.

---

[2] Quoted in Marc Oraison, *Morality for Our Time* (Garden City, New York: Image Books, 1969), p. 22.

Morality can be considered a science, then, because the more human knowledge expands, the more refined mankind's moral sense can become.

Morality is concerned with what ought to be. Morality is not content with just describing things as they are. It is concerned with how things should be. It is interested in how people should act. It calls persons to be more than they are at a given time; it asks them to be better. It requires them to be all that they can be. In this sense, morality is future-directed. It is concerned with the ideal—an ideal possible to live if people would but exert the necessary effort and cooperate with the God-given help available to them.

Morality judges right and wrong in light of what humanity is. In many ways, this is the most important element in Sertillanges' definition. Morality asks people to be the persons they are meant to be. As we have seen, people vary widely on what they think is a proper definition of humankind. An atheistic communist would be content to say that the individual person exists at the whim of the state; right and wrong are determined by what the state says is right and wrong.

A Madison Avenue advertising executive who is trying to sell some cosmetic product would have us believe that people are bodies to be beautified; what is right is to have the sweet-smell cologne, what is wrong is to have body odor.

On the other hand, a Christian would define men and women as children of God with basic dignity and an eternal destiny. What is right is to act as a child of God, what is wrong is to forget one's basic dignity. From a Christian point of view, moral problem-solving is greatly helped by asking the question, "What is the human thing to do?" This is a good question because, as St. Irenaeus put it, "The glory of God is man fully alive."

However, the issue is: *"What is human?"* as opposed to "It's only human" or "To err is human." What is a proper concept of what persons are? Chapter 3 of this book will help give an answer to that question.

A final definition of morality

The final definition of morality is more a description than a definition. It can be summed up in the word *responsibility*. Responsibility has two components, *response* and *ability*. For the Christian, morality is a response to God's incredible, freely given love and his gift of salvation offered to us through our Lord Jesus Christ. It is a "yes" to the free gift of Jesus and the victory over sin and death that he has won for us. Saying "yes" to Jesus means living our lives as his brothers and sisters. Saying "yes" to salvation means living as Jesus would have us live, responding to neighbor, responding to all people, especially those in need. Saying "yes" to Jesus is saying "yes" to his personal invitation to us to live his life in us.

The other side of the coin in Christian morality is the ability to respond to God, the ability to love, the ability to say "yes" to God. Like salvation itself, this ability is a free gift given to us by God. It does not rest primarily on our own talents, strengths, insights or deeds. Rather, it is the gift of the Holy Spirit given to us at baptism. Jesus' Father has given us Christians not only the summons to love, but also the power of God's own love—the Holy Spirit—with which to respond. "The love of God has been poured out in our hearts through the Holy Spirit who has been given to us" (Rom 5:5).

An adequate definition of morality, then, will have the following elements: it is a *science;* concerned about what *ought to be* (norms); *judging right and wrong in light of who we are;* dealing with *human conduct in light of revelation;* summed up by the word *responsibility;* responding to a personal invitation of Jesus.

To think about:

You may have seen the following adjectives: moral, immoral, amoral. When applied to given individuals, they can be distinguished as follows:

moral	One who correctly judges between right and wrong and consequently acts on what is virtuous.
immoral	One who does not act in conformity with accepted principles of right or wrong.
amoral	One who is not concerned with any moral standards at all; such a person does not accept any concept of right or wrong.

Illustrate from either literature, TV or the movies a character who fits each of the words defined above. Discuss what makes that person moral, immoral or amoral.

Christian and Catholic morality

The three definitions of morality given above are all Christian definitions of morality; in fact, they all come from Roman Catholic scholars. Christian morality has its roots in Jesus himself. The thrust of this book will be a morality which accepts the revelation of Jesus. In discussing and applying a method of solving moral problems, it will consciously try to bring in principles of Christian morality. Furthermore, the book is written from the perspective of Roman Catholicism. What this means, in brief, is that the church can and does speak authoritatively and creatively in many areas of morality. A Catholic believes that Jesus entrusted his teaching authority to the church and that the church has the responsibility to offer guidance, help and direction in the solving of moral problems. Where appropriate, the teaching of the church will be consulted in both explaining and applying to specific problems the method of moral decision-making discussed in this book.

SUMMARY

1. Many would agree that our contemporary society has a number of moral problems both personal and social; few can agree on the correct method of solving them.

2. The method of moral decision-making discussed in this book has twelve elements: **S**earch out the facts (what, why, who, where, when and how); **T**hink about the alternatives and consequences; **O**thers, both effects on them and their advice; **P**rayer; Jesus; Reason and Revelation; Imagination; Law; Church; Values; Instinct; Conscience.

3. Morality can be defined as follows:

    a. The science of what man ought to be by reason of what he is.

    b. That part of theology that searches for the norms of free human conduct in light of revelation.

    c. Responsibility (ability to respond to Jesus' personal invitation).

4. Christian morality is rooted in Jesus himself; Catholic morality is Christian morality guided by the teaching authority of the church.

A case to consider: LIFEBOAT morals

Before launching into a discussion of moral problem-solving, you may wish to study and discuss this famous case. (We will return to this case often in the next three chapters for practice in applying the STOP sign.)

A movie entitled *Abandon Ship* depicts in a general way a famous legal case in American law, *U.S. v. Holmes*, 26 Fed. Cases 360 (1842). It tells the story of a ship's captain who decided to sacrifice some lives on a life raft. He did so in the face of severe criticism by some of the passengers and at a personal risk to his own life. The lifeboat could hold at its maximum only 14 people; there were 26 people who survived the shipwreck. The situation became desperate when a severe storm arose. There was no immediate hope of rescue; on the contrary, it looked as if help would come only after a number of days or not at all. His decision in the face of severe protest was to put some of the survivors over the side. They were outfitted with life jackets. His criterion for choosing was the "survival of the fittest." He anticipated that there would be a long hard row to land, a journey of maybe several weeks. Thus, he chose those who had to leave the boat: a man who had inhaled the fumes of fuel oil; an elderly man and his wife, too weak to row the long haul to the coast; a weakened sailor who had not yet reached adulthood; and other people whom he judged weak and infirm. The others in the lifeboat refused to help put the victims over the sides of the boat except at gunpoint. Soon after he put them over the storm ended. Unexpectedly, the lifeboat and its occupants were rescued the next day. All aboard refused to accept responsibility for the captain's actions.

Discussion:

1. Do you agree with the captain's decision? Explain his method of decision-making.

2. Could the other lifeboat occupants rightfully excuse themselves from any responsibility for the actions of the captain?

3. Later on, the captain was tried at court. If you were a jury member, how would you have punished him, if at all?

4. Were there any other ways this dilemma could have been resolved? Discuss.

5. Does any person have the right to take the life of any other person, especially an innocent? Explain and give examples.

6. Can you think of situations similar to this case?

2

The "Stop" Sign

"Fools rush in where angels fear to tread."

The quotes which open the first two chapters make a strong argument for the virtue of prudence in decision-making. The prudent person tries his or her best to make right decisions in matters of conscience. It is true that many decisions we make daily do not take much thought, nor do they demand much time. Which cereal I eat for breakfast, the color of tie I wear, whether I drink coffee or tea, whether I should jog or swim for exercise—all of these are rather routine decisions.

But in matters of right and wrong, decision-making is not always that easy. True, I may know general principles, like "Do good and avoid evil" and "Love your neighbor as yourself," but just what do these mean in a concrete situation? Should I or should I not cheat when everyone else is and the curve on the test is being ruined? Should I go to the party with my friends even when I know for sure that "joints" will be passed around? Should I vote for a particular politician whose views I share except for his stand on abortion? These kinds of questions are more complex and not so easy to decide. They involve thought. They definitely take prudence, wise use of my intelligence and freedom.

27

The next two chapters attempt to present a method of moral decision-making in the Roman Catholic tradition. In explaining the process and giving a number of examples to illustrate it, the process may seem long and involved. In reality, it is not that involved at all. When you get some practice using it, when it becomes part of your mind-set, you will see that many of the steps can be done with lightning speed. Of course, some moral issues are difficult and complex. They take work, investigation, thought and consultation. This method may be helpful in giving some direction to decision-making.

For the sake of review and to help you get a mental picture of the process, the STOP sign is pictured again here. This chapter will explain the S-T-O-P of the moral decision-making method.

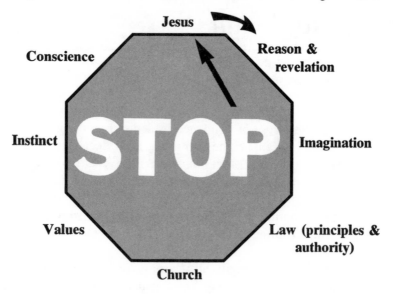

We begin with STOP because in making any kind of decision, we should stop in order to:

> S—SEARCH out the facts
>
> T—THINK about the alternatives and the consequences
>
> O—OTHERS: how do our acts affect them and have we consulted them?
>
> P—PRAY.

SEARCH

The **S** in the STOP sign stands for Search. We should always begin our process of deciding what is right and wrong by searching out the facts. Reporters always ask certain questions in following up a story. These questions are useful for us, too, because as Dr. Maguire points out, they help disclose reality—they are reality-revealing questions. The questions are the five *w's* and the *h*: what, why, who, where, when and how.

WHAT? An excellent starting point in moral decision-making is to know *what* you are talking about. What is it you propose to do? For example, suppose a person is involved in an unwanted pregnancy and is contemplating an abortion. Certainly, before that person should rush into an abortion, she would be wise to know what an abortion is, she would be prudent to realize some basic facts about a fetus. To illustrate: medical science has already shown that at conception the mother and baby are genetically distinct; at 25 days, the baby's heart starts beating; at 30 days, the human brain is formed as well as eyes, ears, mouth, kidneys, liver and umbilical cord; at 45 days, the skeleton is complete and the baby moves for the first time; at 63 days, the baby can grasp an object placed in its hands and make a fist. Looking at pictures of aborted fetuses would also help the person know *what* she is getting into. How is the baby to be aborted? It is generally done one of four ways: The D and C—using a sharp instrument to scrape out the contents of the uterus; salt poisoning which in effect burns the fetus to death; the hysterotomy—cutting into the womb of the mother in order to extract the fetus; and the suction method by which the fetus is forcefully extracted from the womb. These are some of the basic facts someone contemplating abortion should know. In other words, what are you talking about? That is the basic starting point.

What is the morality of premarital sex, that is, sexual activity before marriage? This is a question which has plagued young people (and their elders) for generations. Some people in our society today say the question itself is culturally biased by terming it "premarital," that is to say, that marriage is somehow the ideal against which all sexual activity should be measured. Some would have us ask the question like this: "What is the morality of post-puberty sex?" Regardless of how you phrase the question, you have to ask, "What are you talking about?" Are you talking about passionate glances which can lead to "lusting of the heart"? Are you thinking about handholding? Kissing? Petting? "Going all the way?" To state it another way, without a clear notion of what is meant by "premarital sex," it is difficult to pass judgment on the morality, the rightness and wrongness of it.

Should the United States government spend billions of dollars to develop a neutron bomb? What is a neutron bomb? What kind of damage does it do? Some scientists claim that it is "cleaner" than regular atomic bombs in that it destroys people more than property. The radiation fallout does not seem as potentially dangerous. What does this say about a government which is designing sophisticated weaponry to use against people? Is this issue similar to the issue of whether napalm bombs should have been used in the Vietnam war? Napalm is a gel, which on explosion, sticks to a person's skin and inflicts excruciating, painful burns. It most often harms the old, the infirm and the young who cannot run away from the flying gel fast enough to escape its devastating effects. If a person says to go ahead and develop the neutron bomb or to use napalm, at least the person should realize *what* he or she is talking about.

As another example, consider the morality of cheating. Once again, what do you mean by cheating? Is copying homework from another student considered cheating? On college campuses, there are businesses, engaged in by enterprising people, called "research services." In effect, for a fee, the service will write a term paper on any topic imaginable. If you buy this service and submit a term paper for a course, passing it off as your own, have you cheated? Is it cheating to "borrow" an answer or two from a class-mate during an exam? Is it cheating to take an extra $500 deduction on a federal income tax form? What are you talking about?

Finally, is it wrong to mock someone out? Well, what are you mocking out? Are you gently teasing someone about the way he or she dresses? Or are you attacking someone's religion, his or her sexual orientation, a physical defect, skin color?

The beginning point for any discussion of a moral decision must always be the *what*. It is an important "reality" question because without an answer to it, a person cannot proceed, a person does not know what he or she is deciding. Discovering the *what* sometimes takes work, but it is necessary groundwork for determining right and wrong.

Exercise:

Take the "lifeboat case" given at the end of Chapter 1 and discuss it thoroughly in light of *what?* What are all the important facts? What about shipwrecks? Storms at sea? Survival with limited rations? Line up and discuss as many important features of the *what* that you can think of.

WHY? In morality, *why* is an extremely important question to ask because it gets at the motives of the person performing the action. Motives can make all the difference in morality. Our legal system recognizes this reality. A person who willfully drives a car into a pedestrian crossing the street, doing so coldly and with deliberation, is guilty of first-degree murder; another driver who accidentally hits a person crossing the street after using all due caution surely is not guilty of cold-blooded murder—and the legal system judges accordingly.

Motives in morality were important for Jesus, too. For example, in the parable Jesus told about the Pharisee and the tax collector who went to the Temple to pray, Jesus condemned the Pharisee because of his self-righteousness. On the other hand, Jesus praised the publican who prayed with humility and true sorrow. The publican was justified; the Pharisee was not (Lk 18:9-14).

Thus, the second reality-revealing question is *why*. Notice the difference an answer to the *why* question can make in the following examples. What is the morality of skipping Mass on Sunday? Well, why did you do it? Did you not go to Mass because, on your way to the church, you stopped to help some old people who were having car trouble? Did you do it to shoot a round of golf? Did you do it intentionally to hurt a parent who highly values Sunday worship? Or did you do it out of sheer laziness? Certainly, your motivation is going to affect the rightness and wrongness of not going to Mass.

What about killing someone? Well, once again, what was the motive? Was it done because a person wanted revenge on someone who insulted him or her? Was it done in a fit of rage? Was it done because, generally speaking, the person has no respect for life and thus refuses to obey any traffic laws? Or, perhaps, was it done in self-defense as a last resort after all other measures to protect one's own life had been taken?

Is it right to give money to the poor? We would have to say that in almost every case it is a good thing to give to the poor. But even such an apparently good act is not always right and even the degree of rightness can be affected by the motive. For example, did a person give to the poor out of a genuine concern for the poor and a desire to alleviate their needy condition? Did a person do it with a lot of fanfare so that others would think that he or she is a great human being? Or did the person do it because he or she was trying to relieve some of the guilt left over from cheating a company out of a lot of money? The intention will affect our judgment of this act.

A humorous example points to the real difference motive makes in moral decisions. What is the morality of going to a burlesque show? Is it to see what's going on or is it to see what's coming off? (By the way, this example does *not* suggest that you should go—regardless of the reason.)

Is it all right to lie? What's your motive? Are you doing it to protect the life of a friend who is being threatened unjustly? Are you doing it to protect some highly classified government secrets from a known enemy or someone who clearly has no right to the information? Or are you doing it to cover up real cheating which took place on an examination?

Motives are very important in morality. In the Sermon on the Mount, Jesus called his followers to have only the loftiest intentions. He wants only good motives from his disciples. Thus, when Christians give money to the poor (almsgiving), Jesus says that the right hand should not know what the left is doing. When we pray, we should do it in a way that doesn't call attention to ourselves, not on the street corners for public show like the hypocrites did. When we fast, we should do it with happy faces, not all sad as though we carry the weight of the world on our shoulders in order to get people to think that we are holy (Mt 6:1-18). In other words, in our performance of religious acts, Jesus calls for only the best of motives in his followers. (Incidentally, it is interesting how Jesus in the Sermon on the Mount assumes that his followers will give alms, will pray and fast. He does not try to talk us into doing these good works because he assumes that his followers will do them as a matter of course.)

Our second question then should be "Why do I propose to do this act? What are my motives?" One caution: although we have the obligation in moral decision-making to question our own motives, we should be very, very careful about questioning the motives of others. We simply do not know what others are thinking. Jesus cautioned his disciples about this truth when he said, "If you want to avoid judgment, stop passing judgment" (Mt 7:1). In discussing moral cases and applying the STOP sign, of necessity we have to try to get at intentions and motives, but we should be very reserved about judging the motives of others.

Exercises:

Apply the *why* question to the lifeboat case. Was the captain's intention good? Might he have had ulterior motives? If so, what could some of them have been? Were the intentions of the other lifeboat occupants good in their not assuming any responsibility for what the captain did? Discuss the following:

1. Are good motives sufficient to make an action right?

2. Might an act still be wrong (the *what*) even if the motives are good? Explain and illustrate.

WHO?   In judging moral cases, one should consider the people involved in the situation because they often play a significant role in determining right and wrong. For example, smoking marijuana is a *what* to consider; but an airline pilot (the *who*) "smoking up" will greatly affect the quality of one's judgment of that *what*. It stands to reason that you would not want a pilot "to get high" while embarking on a flight and entrusted with the lives of other people. What's the morality of not keeping a little promise made to someone? Well, who is the someone? Surely, if it is a friend, you might judge the breach of trust a little more severely.

Who is not always a significant question, however. If I rob a man or a woman I have the same result: someone is victimized by theft. The question *who?* should be asked, nevertheless, because it can make all the difference, for example, in the case of stealing from a wealthy person versus a poor person, lying to a friend versus to a total stranger, or foul language used in front of children versus in front of one's "drinking buddies." In all of these cases, the *who* involved can affect the severity of wrongdoing.

WHERE?   Like *who,* the *where* is not always a significant factor. For example, if I rob you downtown or in your own neighborhood, you end up with the same result—you are robbed. But place can often affect the morality of an action. For example, there is nothing inherently wrong with practicing my golf swing, but if I do it in a crowded room of students, I face the real possibility of being charged with assault and battery. Target practice with a .22 caliber gun is all right as long as I confine it to a practice range. A reasonable person would not say that a crowded bus constitutes a practice range. Likewise, loud talking and "goofing around" is great in order to let off steam, but to do it when others are trying to study is definitely out of place because it violates the rights of others.

WHEN? Timing, as well as place and who is involved, need not always be a key factor. If I rob you at 1 A.M., rather than 2 A.M., you are still minus your money. Time, the *when,* is not an important factor here. But a husband demanding his marital rights immediately after his wife has returned home from the hospital following a very difficult and painful operation is surely insensitive. Dating young ladies is fine; dating two weeks after marriage is clearly wrong. Practicing one's trumpet in an apartment house at 3 A.M. is distasteful, if not outright cruel. (Of course, the degree of cruelty depends somewhat on how good a trumpeter you are.) Surely, a teacher has a duty to tell a student that she has failed a course. But, with full knowledge of the events under question, to tell her right after her father has died and she has broken up with her boyfriend is clearly thoughtless—and wrong. Timing is the thing.

To determine the morality of an action, the *who,* the *where* and the *when* must be asked if a person wishes to make an informed judgment on the case under consideration.

Exercises:

Discuss the following questions in relation to the lifeboat case.

1. *Whom* did the captain toss overboard? What was his criterion of choice? Can any person's life be measured by usefulness? Discuss. What is meant by the survival of the fittest? Who determines what is fit? Does anyone have that right?

2. Is the *where* a significant factor in this case?

3. Is the *when* a key factor in this case? Explain. Could the captain's miscalculation of the timing on the rescue have been a major issue here?

HOW? The *how* refers to the *means* used to bring about the desired action. Again, it is not always a significant factor. If I kill you by stabbing you or by poisoning you, the means are not all that important for you—you still have been killed; I have committed murder. But the means are often an extremely important factor in deciding the rightness or wrongness of moral issues. Today, many moral debates concentrate on the means. For example, family planning can be a worthy end, but the means can make a difference. Artificial means of contraception, natural family planning and abortion are different means of achieving the end of family planning. But they are not all moral means. Likewise, deciding to fire an employee from a job may be a desirable end, but the methods used could be humane or cruel and impersonal. Cruelty cannot be justified in order to bring about the desired purpose.

Consider the following: What is the morality of ending a war with atomic weapons? The war may end, it is true, but the world may end, too. Here is a case where the cure is worse than the sickness. May a person save her good reputation by getting an abortion? Clearly, a fine reputation is a desirable thing, but are the means to protect it moral? Relaxation is also good; may I do it by getting "bombed out of my head"? Are the means used to induce relaxation destructive of my humanity? Passing a difficult physics course is quite an achievement; is it moral to cheat in order to pass? May I ease someone's pain (a good intention) by injecting air bubbles into his or her veins in order to bring about instant death (the means)? Should I deal with frustration (it is necessary and good to let off tensions) by taking it out on the family at home?

Considerable help in solving moral problems is offered by a traditional principle in Catholic morality which deals with the *how*. The principle goes like this:

The End Does Not Justify the Means

What is the meaning of the principle "The end does not justify the means"? Simply put, it means that you cannot directly do something that is evil in order to bring about the good effect you are hoping for. A GOOD END DOES NOT JUSTIFY EVIL MEANS TO ACHIEVE IT! The means have to be good or at least neutral to bring about your desired effect. Killing an innocent person is evil; thus, injecting air bubbles into veins—even with the good intention of shortening a very painful terminal illness— would be considered wrong under this solid principle of morality. Dealing with frustration by taking it out on the family would also be an example of using improper means to bring about a desired outcome. Much confusion in solving moral problems can be overcome by applying this valuable principle of Catholic morality.

Exercises:

1. Apply the *how* question to the lifeboat case. Did the means used violate the principle of Catholic morality articulated above? Could you argue that putting certain lifeboat occupants overboard was a neutral means and did not necessarily have to lead to their death?

2. Listed below are several cases. Put a check (√) next to those items which you think violate the "End does not justify the means" principle explained above.

——— a.   Taking a drug to go on a "trip"

——— b.   Taking a drug for a tooth extraction

——— c.   Testing nuclear weapons in the atmosphere for "defense purposes"

——— d.   Driving a car for recreation purposes

——— e.   Driving a car 30 miles over the speed limit for recreation purposes

——— f.   Burning the American flag to protest racial injustice

——— g.   Picketing the Russian embassy to protest Soviet persecution of Jews

——— h.   Stealing from the rich to give to the poor

3. In the cases listed above, how important is the *what,* the *why,* the *who,* the *when* and the *where?* Explain and discuss.

SUMMARY

Searching out the facts in moral problems implies asking basic reality questions, questions which correspond to the five *w's* and the *h.* In more traditional terminology, each of the reality questions corresponds to concepts in Catholic morality. They are as follows:

what .... the moral object
                                        (what is being done)

why .... intention (motive)

who, where,
when and how .... circumstances (the situation)

In traditional language, then, every moral problem consists of the moral object, that is, the action being contemplated; the intention of the actor, that is, the motive the one doing the act has in mind when performing it; and the various circumstances which give color and texture to the moral object. These three elements, in conclusion, give rise to another extremely important principle in Catholic morality. This principle is stated simply below:

> *If any of the elements in a moral case are evil* (the moral object—what one does; the intention; or the circumstances), *the action itself should be considered wrong.*

Thus, if your intention is good and the circumstances are OK, but if *what* you are doing is clearly inhuman (like rape), then the action is wrong. If the what is OK (like walking to the bank) and the circumstances are all right, but the intention is wrong (for example, the reason you are walking to the bank is to rob it), the action then becomes wrong. Finally, if the moral object and intention are all right but one of the circumstances is out of place, then once again the action becomes wrong. For example, exploding firecrackers in a crowd of people is wrong even if there is nothing wrong with setting them off (the what), nor with having a good time (the intention); what makes this wrong is the place (the circumstances).

Exercises:

Which reality-revealing question do you think is most important in each of the following cases? Write the proper question in the space provided. Share with your classmates and discuss.

—— 1. Habitually doing no homework out of laziness

—— 2. "Cussing" in front of children

—— 3. Mocking out a classmate

—— 4. Making fun of a priest

—— 5. Failing to give money to the missions

—— 6. Going to racially segregated private schools

—— 7. Swimming alone in an unguarded pool

—— 8. Eating $1 worth of junk food for lunch

—— 9. Profaning God's name

—— 10. Missing Mass on Sunday three times a year

—— 11. A married man reading sexually stimulating material

—— 12. Selling sexually stimulating material to minors

—— 13. Littering the highways

—— 14. Paying a compliment to someone within earshot of others

—— 15. Correcting someone by sarcasm

In the space provided below, write up a brief case for each of the following situations:

1. Motives and circumstances are OK; moral object is evil:

2. What and circumstances are OK; motive is evil:

3. What and why are fine; a circumstance is evil:

THINK

The **T** in the STOP sign means Think. After searching out the basic facts of particular moral cases, it is necessary to reflect more deeply on them before making a decision. This deeper reflection includes two very important steps: 1) considering alternatives to the proposed action; 2) reflecting on the consequences of the action.

CONSIDERING ALTERNATIVES. Life is rarely so simple (or complex, for that matter) that there has to be just one particular way of doing something. Human creativity and inventiveness can usually discover multiple ways of approaching the same issue, the same problem. As a matter of fact, human intelligence demands that we at least look at different approaches to a given problem. When confronted with difficult decisions, a good way to get the courage to decide is to look at the problem from many different angles. Even if the alternatives are not all that good, at least we can say that the solution we end up with was arrived at by examining all the evidence, all the approaches.

There is an ancient proverb which sheds light on this reality of considering alternatives. Truth is compared to an elephant; those pursuing the truth are like blind men. Several of them try to get at the truth: one grabs hold of the elephant's tail; another puts his arms around a leg; still another touches the trunk. Each blind man tries to describe the elephant from his vantage point. Each has part of the truth, but no one can see the whole elephant. Until they either see the whole or get a grasp of the various parts of the elephant, they will not begin to know what an elephant (or truth) is. So it is with moral problems. Until we look at them from many vantage points, we will not realize that there just might be another way to solve the problem.

For example, take the woman who is contemplating abortion. Assume that she has searched out the facts. She knows the what of abortion; she has examined her motives; she knows the other facts involved. But has she considered the alternatives? Must she abort? What about the possibility of adoption? Is she aware that there are many couples who wait a long time to adopt babies but cannot because there are so few available. What about an organization like Birthright which will help her bring the baby to term and give her the moral (and often financial) support to lessen her personal trauma? Birthright is a humane alternative to abortion and a very good one, too. Homes for unwed mothers are a possibility. They may not be a good possibility for a given woman, but at least they should be considered. What about marriage? This is probably a very bad alternative because the vast majority of teen marriages end in divorce. Some statistics say that around 90 percent of those who marry before age 18 end in divorce. There are tragic statistics that seem to eliminate marriage as a real alternative to abortion—but at least it should be considered.

Take the issue of drinking to get drunk. Why do people do it? Many use the excuse that it is the only way to have a good time. Is it, though? Might this not indicate a lack of creativity or a lack of intelligence? Need a person get "bombed" to have a good time? Are there not other ways to enjoy other people's company, to break down barriers to communication between people? Drinking is certainly not the only way to have a good time, nor is it the only way to release tensions. If it were, then maybe the moral issue would be different; but because there are alternatives, drinking and drug-taking are indeed moral problems.

Is cheating the only way to pass an exam? Some people say it is, when the teacher is unfair. Has he or she been talked to? If that does not resolve the problem, what about a conference with the department chairperson, the principal? What about a delegation of students talking to the teacher? Could parents help? Could real hard study help? Maybe none of these will be followed up, but the real issue is: have they been considered?

Premarital sex is a moral issue. Must every date end up with heavy necking, for example? The problem with heavy necking and petting is that sex is like war—it tends to escalate. Someone once said it is a lot like eating potato chips—you can't just have one.

Well, what are the alternatives? Have the people involved thought that there is more to male-female relationships than just sex? What about building up the friendship? Has double-dating been considered? What about avoiding those occasions and places which past experience shows are dangerous?

Should the American government pay farmers not to farm certain lands so the economy will not be upset by large surpluses? This is a complex social justice issue. The starting point is always to search out the facts. What is the issue? Why? Who is involved? Where? When? How? But, also, what are the alternatives? Just to mention one, what would prevent the government from buying surpluses from the farmers and giving them to the poor of this country and other nations? Perhaps it is not desirable for the government to make direct handouts to other governments. Well, could the surpluses be given to church groups to distribute? If not, what are the alternatives? In other words, is paying the farmers not to plant the only solution to surplus crops?

Exercises:

Consider the lifeboat case. Listed below are some alternatives to what the captain did. Discuss whether you think any of these are realistic in light of the case as you discussed it so far.

- He could have let everyone stay in the boat.
- He could have asked for volunteers to sacrifice their places in the boat.
- The occupants could have drawn lots. (By the way, this is the course of action suggested by the Court in the case *U.S. v. Holmes.*)
- Survivors could have taken turns floating and then occupying the lifeboat.
- A certain number could have been put in the water but holding lifelines attached to the boat.
- The strong ones could have been put over the sides instead of the weak ones.

Can you list any other alternatives? Discuss each in turn.

REFLECTING ON THE CONSEQUENCES. Every act has certain consequences: some of them can be foreseen; others cannot. A reflection on the consequences, the results of our actions, is a powerful help in judging the rightness or wrongness of those acts. Traditionally, however, Catholic morality has refused to put all the emphasis on the consequences. As we shall see more clearly in Chapter 3, our acts themselves are powerful indicators of who we are—they help reveal our identity. Even good results cannot justify evil actions, as we saw above. Our deeds have significance in themselves and they tell us about ourselves. Thus, we make or break our lives by the deeds we either choose to do or not to do. Although the effects of the deeds are important, they do not have primary importance. With this said, though, we should look at the results of our acts because the consequences are part of the total reality of *what* we are doing. They help us decide on the right and the wrong in a given situation.

For example, what are the effects of shoplifting? It may seem like a "small" crime which "everyone does," but in reality it is a big problem that affects all consumers by causing higher prices. Many people are forced to pay the cost of the crimes of a few.

Or take the case of governments encouraging a policy of freeway development. Pouring money into more and more miles of concrete ribbon can have a number of undesirable effects. For example, there is less money available for the development of public transportation systems, the major means of transportation for the poor. Second, because of the ease of transportation to places of work, it certainly encourages people to move out of the central city, leading to a draining away of money and people from an area that needs strong economic and human resources to survive. Third, it does little to discourage the serious air pollution problem and often directly leads to an increase in it.

Surely, many people would say that driving a car to work is not a moral problem. Is this true? Consider the consequences. Is driving the car absolutely necessary? What about car-pooling? Science has documented well the ill effects of automobile pollutants. How are we upsetting the ecological balance today, thus causing problems for our children and grandchildren in years to come? Might we not be hurting our genes and chromosomes, thus contributing to cancer and diseases yet to be named? What is the effect of wasteful consumption of the world's energy supplies on the rest of the world? Is there or is there not an energy crisis? What do right and wrong have to do with the fact that eight percent of the world's population disproportionately consumes 35 percent of the world's material goods? Driving a car needlessly is part of these larger moral issues.

What is the result of social drinking? It can lead to driving while under the influence of alcohol, thus endangering the lives of innocent people. It can lead to addiction and a life of great sorrow and pain involving not only the individual but also one's family, co-workers and friends.

What about a simple act of cheating on a test? What effect does it have on the curve? On fellow students? On the teacher's attitude to the class? Do not acts of cheating make you a cheater? Can they not, in a real sense, change who you are?

Does indulging in premarital sex perhaps not have the effect of closing one's self off to truly loving a person? Cannot a lack of self-control in sexual matters before marriage contribute to a lack of faithfulness to one's partner after marriage? Might not these acts be selfish, thus possibly hurting others? What happens if sexual abuses are tolerated in society as a whole—something that seems to be happening in our contemporary American society? Does this kind of looseness of morals lead to pornography, acceptance of all kinds of bizarre behavior, the breakdown of family life, the lack of respect for the uniqueness of individuals? All of these are possible consequences and thus should be reflected on in the making of moral decisions.

Exercises:

1. List and discuss all the possible consequences of the captain's decision in the lifeboat case. Discuss the consequences of each of the captain's alternatives as found in the exercises on p. 43.

2. List and discuss as many consequences as possible to the following cases:

   a. Shoplifting from a large supermarket

   b. Prolonging a person's life on machines and tubes

   c. Refusing to fight in a war

   d. Excluding certain racial groups from a neighborhood

   e. Gossiping about a fellow student.

OTHERS

In the STOP sign, **O** stands for other people. One undeniable fact about human life is that humans are social beings. We are dependent on others for our very life, for our education, for our employment, for most aspects of everyday living. We are beings who live with others; moreover, the Christian believes that we live for others as well. Consequently, in making moral decisions, other people should hold a key place in our arriving at a decision to do right or wrong. Part of the reflection on the consequences of our actions is a serious consideration of how they will affect other people. Secondly, because we are social beings, it is often prudent to ask for and reflect on the advice of others.

HOW OUR ACTIONS AFFECT OTHERS. Take a simple example like smoking cigarettes. Few people would consider this a moral issue. Are they correct? What might be the effect of my smoking on others? Do I contribute to the bad health of others by smoking in their presence? In light of the scientific evidence which reports that smoking has a very good chance to lessen the length of my life, is it fair to those I love to continue to smoke?

Am I depriving them of a brother or a sister, a son or a daughter, a father or a mother? In no way can smoking be seen as something that just concerns me.

How does the pollution of our streams and lakes deprive others of the crystal-clear, healthful water so necessary for life? Here we should consider not only this generation but all future generations as well.

How might an inordinate preoccupation over material things make me selfish and consequently less open to other people, especially the poor? Even my secret thoughts have a social effect in that they can either tend to open or close me to others.

Related to this issue is the American custom of spending close to 20 billion dollars a year on liquor and tobacco. Contrast this with the frightening fact that approximately two people per minute die of starvation every day. We are all aware of the harmful effects of liquor and tobacco, both luxuries. But do we know what it means to die of starvation? *Time* magazine reports that the victim of starvation literally burns up his or her own body fats, muscles and tissues for fuel. The body consumes itself and deteriorates rapidly. The kidneys, liver and endocrine system often cease to function properly. The mind ceases to function clearly because of the lack of carbohydrates, necessary in brain chemistry. Confusion sets in; victims often seem unaware of their plight. The body is prone to disease which most often kills the victims of famine. A person begins to starve when he or she has lost a third of his or her normal body weight. Once the loss exceeds 40 percent, death is almost inevitable. In the face of these horrifying facts, one can only wonder whether our money could not be spent more wisely for others than on self-indulgence.

A final example might be the modern issue from medical morality known as cloning. Cloning is the asexual reproduction of an exact duplicate of a member of some species. Scientists claim that within several generations, if not sooner, humans can be cloned. If it becomes possible, does that mean it should be done? Another name for this is the "can-do" fallacy. Just because science "can do" something does not mean that it morally ought to do it. What effect will this have on people? Especially what will it say about married love and procreative reproduction? Might mankind not be reduced to an animalistic—or even mechanical— level of existence? This is a serious possibility that must be considered.

CONSULTING OTHERS. The wise person rarely goes it alone. Even the experienced writer asks some competent person to check his or her work. Doctors often get a second or third opinion in the diagnosis of an extremely difficult medical case. Other knowledgeable people do the same. Making moral decisions is no different. At times, it is very prudent to discuss one's decision with another. We do not live in a vacuum. It is the humble person who can admit that he or she does not have the wisdom of Solomon and is willing to dig deeper for other points of view.

A number of people can be sources of great help in making moral decisions. Certainly, those wiser and more experienced than we are can be of much help. Parents and adults have the wisdom of age and experience; their viewpoint is invaluable. Teachers and counselors are usually willing to offer their suggestions. Priests can give many helpful suggestions and guidelines based on their training and vocation. Books and articles usually are the result of much research and offer good guidance in matters of morality. Our friends especially can be helpful in "leveling with us" and telling us if we are deceiving ourselves. Because they know us so well, friends can help point out our blind spots in our moral reasoning. All these and others can give us much aid in the making of moral decisions.

A person thinking about joining a demonstration against nuclear weapons may wish to talk with other protestors who have engaged in this kind of activity. He or she may check out with other concerned citizens who do not engage in marches about the "tactical wisdom" of demonstrations. The kinds of questions that might be asked would include: "Do marches accomplish more good than harm? Are there other ways to register protest and yet still affect the decision-making process? What are the risks involved in marching? What are the risks involved in not publicly registering protest?"

Those thinking about engaging in premarital sex might ask parents and teachers why they caution young people about intimate relations before marriage. There must be something to the various values older generations put on purity and chastity. Often much wisdom is found in these standards. It is the foolish person who would simply dismiss these norms as "old-fashioned" without trying to find out the reasons behind them.

The cautions society puts on drinking and drugs is also worthy of consultation and reflection. For example, it is often eye-opening to talk to a reformed addict or an alcoholic about his or her experience. It is not necessary for each generation to reinvent the wheel when there are those who can pass on the discoveries of the past. The issue is the same in the area of deciding right and wrong. Checking out the experiences of others can be a great help in choosing and then doing the right thing.

Exercises:

Apply the O to the lifeboat case. You might discuss these questions:

1. Was the captain in a position to check out his experiences with anyone else? Explain.

2. What were some of the effects on others of his decision? If his decision were upheld by the court, what might be the effect of his action on people in similar situations in the future? Were those on the lifeboat the only ones affected by his actions? Explain.

PRAY

The **P** in the STOP sign signifies prayer. When the sweat and hard work of searching, thinking and considering others is completed, in a sense, one's task is really only half begun. For the Christian, prayer is a powerful way to get God's help in searching out his will for us. In its simplest form, prayer is putting oneself consciously in the presence of the Lord. A principle of our faith is that he is intimately concerned with how we live our lives, that he is very interested in us as individuals. "As for you, every hair of your head has been counted; so do not be afraid of anything" (Mt 10:30-31). He promised that he would be with us and help us in our daily living. "If you, with all your sins, know how to give your children good things, how much more will the heavenly Father give the Holy Spirit to those who ask him" (Lk 11:13).

There are many ways to pray; there are different paths to finding out God's will. Four of them will be mentioned briefly here. The first flows from a promise Jesus himself made and it involves others:

> Again I tell you, if two of you join your voices on earth to pray for anything whatever, it shall be granted you by my Father in heaven. Where two or three are gathered in my name, there am I in their midst (Mt 18: 19-20).

As we have discussed in the previous section, consulting others can be helpful in making moral decisions. Praying with others in Jesus' name is also worthy of our consideration. Imagine a married couple trying to decide if they should have another child. They have searched, they have considered alternatives and consequences, they have thought about and talked to others. Together, they could pray and ask for our Lord's help and guidance in this often difficult decision.

Another form of prayer is meditation. Meditation is a deep reflection on something in the presence of the Lord. Many Christians meditate with scripture. Our faith is that scripture is a living word of God, a word that still speaks to his people today. For example, suppose a person is trying to decide what to do with some money which came as a windfall. The person seriously desires to do the right thing and really does not want to be corrupted by the money. He or she may read several sayings of Jesus on the topic of money and reflect on the words. (Examples here might include Mt 25:31-46, Lk 16:19-31 and Lk 16:9-15.)

Although we must guard against overly simplistic interpretations of scriptures, a reflection on them can be a powerful guide to doing right. Perhaps after reading and meditating on the above passages, the person with the windfall may take a Caribbean cruise, but only after donating a certain sum of money to his or her favorite charity. One sign that money does not have an enslaving hold on a person is that he or she is able to give some of it away.

Reflection on events in our lives in the presence of the Lord is a method of prayer. The Christian believes in divine providence, that God the Father is concerned about and watches over his children. Can we find a reason why we are in a given place at a given time? Why are certain people sent into our lives? Why did these things happen to us? Why have we been given certain talents? These are the kinds of prayerful questions that Christians might ask themselves. Like the Jews who contemplated the marvelous things Yahweh did for them in their history, we also believe that God works in our personal history. For example, is it merely accidental that you are reading this book on morality? Perhaps you have read something already or will read something that will help you do good things not only for yourself but for others. Perhaps a question has been asked that has given you pause to think about something you never considered before. Maybe something has happened to you already that—if you reflect on it—may help you decide the right thing in a similar situation. This kind of prayerful reflection is extremely helpful in making moral decisions.

The fourth reality about prayer that we should never forget is that our Lord encourages us to ask for things in his name and that those prayers will always be answered.

In this regard, read Lk 11:1-13. The point of this passage is that we might have to be persistent but that the Father will always give us the help we seek, he will always do the good thing for us. Surely, he would never turn down the sincere request for guidance in choosing the right thing to do. This guidance may come in different forms: in a sense of peacefulness that I am doing the right thing; in a fresh insight that I never had before; in a person who says something or does something that helps me look at the issue in a different way; in a feeling of "wait and see"; in the courage to make and follow through on a decision which demands prompt action.

Prayer is a good way to end this discussion of the STOP sign. In our discussion of a method for making moral decisions, prayer is a transitional point. It leads us to a discussion of the points around the octagon; that discussion begins with Jesus. All prayer ultimately is joined to our Lord: a consideration of his person and his teaching is an important stage for the Christian who is trying to make a moral decision.

Exercises:

1. In the lifeboat case, was it practical for the captain to pray? Was it practical for him not to have prayed? Explain and discuss your answer.

2. Survey at least two classmates and three adults and ask them these questions. Share the results of your findings.

        a. Do you pray before making an important decision?

        b. If you do pray, how do you pray? Why?

        c. Has prayer ever helped you in making a decision to do the right thing? Explain.

SUMMARY

1. This chapter explained and exemplified half of the process of the moral decision-making method known as the STOP sign. It involves asking the following questions and taking the following steps.

S-earching: *What* do I propose to do?
Why—what are my motives?
Who is involved?
Where?
When?
How?

T-hinking: What are the *alternatives* to what I propose to do?
What are the *consequences* of my action?

O-thers: How does what I propose to do *affect* others?
Have I *consulted* others?

P-ray: Have I prayed?

2. The chapter explained two important principles of Catholic morality:

a. The end does not justify the means. (A good end does not justify evil means to achieve it.)

b. If any of the elements in a moral case are evil (the moral object—what one does; the motives; or the circumstances), the action itself should be considered wrong.

Exercises:

Apply the steps in the **S-T-O-P** of the **STOP** sign to the following case. Discuss thoroughly with your classmates.

Scenario: Tom and Jack are good friends. Tom discovers that Jack is a drug pusher, a pusher of pills. Jack sells to high school kids and also to kids in junior high. His argument is that the kids know what the effects of the drugs are, and this relieves him of any responsibility.

Tom is quite disturbed by his friend's behavior. He seeks advice from his friend Jim who claims that Tom should not turn Jack in. Why? Because that would be meddling in something that does not concern him; furthermore, it would be betraying a friend. In addition, what good would it do? The kids who use drugs would just get them from somebody else.

Tom's girlfriend also thinks it would be a bad scene for him to turn Jack in to the authorities. The worst thing a person can do is to betray a friend.

On confronting Jack, Tom learns that he is willing to stop pushing after he gets rid of his current supply. But Tom is not at all convinced. He is in a real turmoil. What should he do?

Some questions:

1. To whom does Tom owe the greatest responsibility— his friend or those who might purchase pills from him? Whose welfare should he be most concerned about? What if Jack had been his brother?

2. Why is there such a strong feeling that one should never tell on a friend?

3. Does Tom have a *right* to interfere in Jack's affairs? An *obligation?* What are some of the alternatives available to him to stop Jack? Some of the consequences if he does or does not?

4. When does someone have the responsibility to interfere in someone else's life? What about the responsibility when that behavior is legal and widely approved of? (E.g., abortion.) What guidelines would you establish in answering this question?

5. Is it the seller's or buyer's responsibility if the buyer suffers some ill effects? What about the age of the buyer?

6. Refer to the moral positions discussed on pages 10 and 11 of Chapter 1. How might each of these solve this problem?

3

The STOP Sign, Continued

Two others who were criminals were led along with him to be crucified.

When they came to Skull Place, as it was called, they crucified him there and the criminals as well, one on his right and the other on his left. [Jesus said, "Father, forgive them; they do not know what they are doing."] They divided his garments, rolling dice for them (Lk 23:32-34).

The last chapter began a discussion on how to solve moral problems. The process for moral decision-making must begin with searching out the facts, thinking about the alternatives and the consequences, considering and consulting others and praying. This chapter will take the process a bit further by discussing other factors which should be taken into consideration in studying moral problems. We begin our discussion of the elements around the STOP sign by focusing on the heart of Christian morality, the teaching of Jesus.

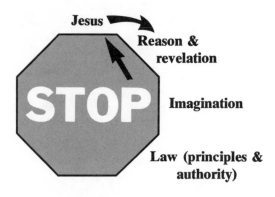

Jesus

Reason &
revelation

Imagination

Law (principles &
authority)

JESUS

Anyone who is trying to do the right thing from a Christian perspective will ultimately have to ask the question "What would Jesus want me to do?" This is an easy question to ask but a much more difficult one to answer. At times it is a difficult question to answer because Jesus did not teach a systematic code of ethics which provides neat answers to all moral issues that may ever come up in human affairs. Unlike some of the Jewish scribes and lawyers of his day, Jesus did not hand down a fully developed collection of laws and a commentary on them for his disciples to follow exactly. There are many moral issues that Jesus never addressed either because questions were not put to him or because they were not problems in his day.

Jesus was asked about divorce, so he provided an answer. He restored his Father's original law, that is when man and woman are joined together, they should never divorce. "What I say to you is: everyone who divorces his wife . . . forces her to commit adultery" (Mt 5:32). Jesus was also asked about the morality of paying money to the foreign government which often cruelly taxed the subjugated Jewish nation. His answer was an indirect one which in effect told his questioners to figure out the answer for themselves: "Give to Caesar what is Caesar's, but give to God what is God's" (Mk 12:17). On the other hand, when it comes to questions like the morality of artificial insemination, cloning, atomic warfare, artificial means of birth control and genetic manipulation, you cannot find the Jesus of the New Testament uttering a word about these topics.

Does Jesus' silence on so many moral issues of burning concern today mean that he has no relevance to us in our attempt to solve complex moral problems? Many times, Christians wish they could turn to the New Testament and find out exactly what they should do on particular issues. In not finding answers there, some people conclude that there is very little guidance Jesus has offered men and women today in their attempts to do the right thing. This conclusion, however, is very far from the truth. Our faith tells us that Jesus is the Risen Lord who—through his Spirit—lives within us to guide us both as a community and as individuals to his Father. His life within us gives us the power and ability to discover and to do his Father's will.

When we unite ourselves to Jesus and read his word in the New Testament, in a spirit of prayer and open to his good news, we can receive powerful insights that can make all the difference in solving moral problems. These insights and truths, which are the heart of Jesus' ethical teaching, can be summarized in two simple questions that must always be asked about whatever actions we propose to do. They are: Is what we propose to do a loving thing? Does what we propose to do tend to serve others? In a way, these two questions are asking the same thing. Let us examine them a little more closely.

Is this a loving thing? For Jesus, and for his followers, all morality is summarized in the Golden Rule: "Treat others the way you would have them treat you: this sums up the law and the prophets" (Mt 7:12). Another way of stating the same thing is:

> You shall love the Lord your God
> with all your heart,
> with all your soul,
> with all your strength,
> and with all your mind;
> and your neighbor as yourself (Lk 10:27).

The basis of the moral code of Jesus, then, is to love. The Beatles some years back sang "All you need is love." Were the Beatles and Jesus saying the same thing? It seems so simple, so basic; and, yet, is it? For example, it is one thing to act out of a loving disposition, out of a loving motive (like wanting to do a loving thing for another). It is quite another thing actually to do the loving thing itself. Abortion is a good example. A person may advocate an abortion out of love for the mother, but the action itself is not very loving for the child. Wanting to love must be translated into doing love.

Unfortunately, much of what passes for love is not what Jesus was talking about. There are different kinds of love. So-called "free-love"—another term for unbridled sexual self-indulgence—is certainly not the same thing as a mother sacrificing for her children or a person dying to save the life of another.

The Greeks distinguished among four different kinds of love. One kind of love is the destructive self-love of the mythological youth Narcissus. You might remember the story. Narcissus was an extremely handsome young man who went to a spring of water one day to look at his reflection. He fell in love with his image so much that he could not take his eyes off himself, and was transformed into the flower that bears his name. This kind of love, known as narcissism, is destructive and is not the kind of love of which Jesus spoke.

Eros is another kind of love the Greeks distinguished. It refers to the passionate attraction between the sexes. This is a necessary and good love. It is the kind of love that C.S. Lewis said that lovers are in. "I'm in love" is a good kind of love, but it does not capture the reality of the love Jesus is talking about here.

Nor does the Greek term for friendship, *philia,* adequately describe what Christian love is all about. Friendship love is very important in human relationships, but it is not quite the same thing as "loving your neighbor as yourself."

This last kind of love is what Jesus spoke of and in the Greek is known as *agape*. Fr. Charles Curran defines agape-love as "the loving concern which is a total giving independent of the lovable qualities of the other."[1] This is the quality of love which should characterize the love of Christians in their actions toward others.

Loving God above all things essentially means adoring him with gratitude for all that he has given to us; loving our neighbor as ourselves means creative giving and forgiving of the other. How do we know we are loving? St. Paul gives us a hint in his great passage on love found in 1 Cor 13:4-7. There, Paul writes that:

> Love is patient; love is kind. Love is not jealous, it does not put on airs, it is not snobbish. Love is never rude, it is not self-seeking, it is not prone to anger; neither does it brood over injuries. Love does not rejoice in what is wrong but rejoices with the truth. There is no limit to love's forbearance, to its trust, its hope, its power to endure.

Paul further drives this home in Colossians where he admonishes us to be who we are. Not to love will be repugnant to us because it will deny our true identity.

> Because you are God's chosen ones, holy and beloved, clothe yourselves with heartfelt mercy, with kindness, humility, meekness, and patience. Bear with one another; forgive whatever grievances you have against one another. Forgive as the Lord has forgiven you. Over all these virtues put on love, which binds the rest together and makes them perfect. Christ's peace must reign in your hearts, since as members of the one body you have been called to that peace. Dedicate yourselves to thankfulness. Let the word of Christ, rich as it is, dwell in you. In wisdom made perfect, instruct and admonish one another. Sing gratefully to God from your hearts in psalms, hymns, and inspired songs. Whatever you do, whether in speech or in action, do it in the name of the Lord Jesus (Col 3:12-17a).

---

[1] Charles E. Curran, *Themes in Fundamental Moral Theology* (Notre Dame: University of Notre Dame Press, 1977), p. 8.

For the Christian, to act morally is to love one's neighbor. Who is our neighbor? Jesus told the parable of the Good Samaritan (Lk 10:29-37) to indicate that everyone is our neighbor, especially the poor, children, sinners, the one who needs us the most and even our enemies. Jesus said that we would be judged based on how we related to those who are the least among us:

> The king will say to those on his right: "Come. You have my Father's blessing! Inherit the kingdom prepared for you from the creation of the world. For I was hungry and you gave me food, I was thirsty and you gave me drink. I was a stranger and you welcomed me, naked and you clothed me. I was ill and you comforted me, in prison and you came to visit me." . . . "I assure you, as often as you did it for one of my least brothers, you did it for me" (Mt 25:34-36; 40).

One of the first questions we should ask, then, about any action and whether it is right or wrong is: Is this loving? For example, is aborting a baby a loving thing to do? Might not fetal life be among the "least of these" Jesus refers to in Matthew's Gospel? Are discrimination and prejudice moral, for example, by refusing to allow certain racial or religious groups to move into our neighborhood? Well, is it loving? Who is our neighbor? Is getting back at someone who hurt us moral? What would St. Paul say? Is it, in the last analysis, loving?

Love of neighbor involves, then, building up the community, building up God's kingdom. A central focus in morality is this dimension of community, of considering the needs of others, no matter who these others are. Community is a product of love— it is a unity created by caring, sharing and being concerned about others.

Is this a serving thing? A second question we could ask ourselves before making moral decisions concerns service of others. In reality, service is a kind of love. We have the words of Jesus himself:

> You know how among the Gentiles those who seem
> to exercise authority lord it over them; their great
> ones make their importance felt. It cannot be like
> that with you. Anyone among you who aspires to
> greatness must serve the rest; whoever wants to rank
> first among you must serve the needs of all. The
> Son of Man has not come to be served but to
> serve—to give his life in ransom for the many
> (Mk 10:42-45).

In addition, the example of Jesus in John's Gospel is especially
illustrative (Jn 13:1-17). There he washed the feet of the apostles
to show that his followers should be motivated by an attitude of
what they can do for others, not what they can get from them.
Every Christian is primarily a foot-washer, a doer, an active agent
of God's love in the world. The attitude of a Christian is not one of
only avoiding doing harm to others; it is also one of asking: What
can I do to help? How can I be like the Lord who went around
doing for others?

Applying this insight of service to contemporary moral issues,
what might one answer to these kinds of questions? How is an act
of premarital sex serving the other? How does my cheating serve
others? How does exploiting the environment serve others? Does
this lie help others? Does absenting myself from Sunday Mass
serve others? Does my foul language help anyone?

If I discover that my answer to these kinds of questions is that
the proposed action is in reality a disservice, then I ought not do
the action.

Following Jesus is hard work. Living a Christian moral life
is demanding. It implies that we ask some really hard questions,
questions such as: Am I loving? Am I serving others by what I am
doing? However, when we honestly ask and then respond to these
two questions, we are very often able to sift through the confusion
of moral problems. It was not easy for Jesus to hang on the Cross
and forgive his persecutors. But, by so doing, he loved us, he
served us, he won for us our redemption. What he did was the
supreme example of a moral act. He calls all his followers to do
the same kind of thing in daily living.

For Further Study, Reflection and Discussion:

1. Apply what you learned in this section (Is it loving? Does it serve others?) to the lifeboat case and the Tom and Jack case introduced at the end of the last chapter.

2. MONEY AND YOU

   How do you react to the following familiar statements? Mark them SA for "strongly agree"; A for "agree"; D for "disagree"; and SD for "strongly disagree."

   ———— Money is the root of all evil.

   ———— The love of money is the root of all evil.

   ———— Money talks.

   ———— Money can't buy everything.

   ———— The poor you will have with you always.

   ———— If you don't watch out for yourself, no one else will.

   ———— The rich get richer and the poor get poorer.

   ———— Money isn't everything; health is two percent.

Our attitudes toward money and wealth can greatly influence our choices in life both in regard to other people and our own vocation. Jesus said a number of things about money. Check out the following references:

- "Then give to Caesar what is Caesar's, but give to God what is God's" (Lk 20:25). (On the question posed by the opponents of Jesus concerning taxation.)

- "How hard it will be for the rich to go into the Kingdom of God! Indeed, it is easier for a camel to go through a needle's eye than for a rich man to enter the kingdom of heaven" (Lk 18:24-25). (Jesus said this about wealth after a rich young man turned down Jesus' invitation to follow him. The young man refused to sell his riches and give them to the poor.)

- "No servant can serve two masters. Either he will hate the one and love the other or be attentive to the one and despise the other. You cannot give yourself to God and money" (Lk 16:13). (Jesus' teaching on wealth after his parable on the "Wily Manager.")

Discuss:

a. Does Jesus ask his followers to be poor? Explain.

b. If you are blessed with good things, what are you supposed to do?

c. What does it mean to be poor in spirit?

d. How do you know if money is starting to control your life?

REASON AND REVELATION

An excellent guide in doing the right thing is to do the human thing. That is such a simple statement to make. Morality and ethics would be a simple task if only everyone knew and agreed upon what the human thing was. Unfortunately, it is not that easy. Not everyone agrees on a common definition of what a human is, so not everyone is going to say that a given action is good or that another action is bad. If it is human it is good; if it is inhuman it is bad. We are left with the question, what does it mean to be human?

A superficial biological answer to the question is relatively easy. Man belongs to the species *Homo sapiens.* He is not that lovely a creature. He walks upright, is prone to fight, likes to talk a lot and, among the many species on this planet, is certainly not the strongest. His young are helpless longer than the young of any other species. He seems to be among the worst adapted of all the animals. He has little hair and consequently has trouble coping with the cold. His eyesight is relatively weak; his sense of smell can only pick out the strongest odors. He cannot run long distances and tires easily. He has difficulty climbing trees and digging holes. He cannot live under the water and is a poor swimmer. He cannot fly, nor can he jump very high. Left unaided, he has difficulty protecting himself or killing for food. It is a wonder that he has survived at all.

A biological answer to what it means to be human is obviously not enough for a person seeking the right thing to do. Our definition of what a human person is must go beyond mere scientific observation. We sense this when in popular speech we say such things as: "He acted like a beast when he told her off." "In his drunken state, he was an animal." "Her mind was so far gone that she was a vegetable." These are not nice things to say about people but they do tell us something about moral judgments made about them. Acting like a beast or an animal or being like a vegetable is somehow saying that a person is inhuman. *To be moral is to be human.* And to be truly human is to be moral. Being what you are and acting as you should as a member of the human race is what morality is all about. Let us now turn to what human reason and divine revelation have to offer in the solution of this problem.

HUMAN REASON REVEALS SOMETHING ABOUT WHO WE ARE. Two short sentences can get at a definition of the human based on what our reason reveals to us.

1. Humans are spiritual-material beings. Various philosophers through the ages have expressed this in different ways. For example, Aristotle defined man as "a rational animal." This is a weak definition because perhaps it places too much emphasis on man's rational nature and not enough on other aspects of our being. For many centuries, humans were described as beings with a body and a soul. This is a good definition but it too is a bit weak because it somewhat gives the impression that we have split personalities. In reality, human life is a single whole; we are not only bodies with souls, we are souls with bodies. A better way to put it is that we are spiritual-material beings. What does this mean?

• *We can think.* Although some animals (like porpoises and higher primates) demonstrate advanced levels of instinct and even rudimentary attempts at thought, none of them has given any evidence that they can reflect, meditate or create. One thing that separates us from plant and animal life is that we know that we know. We can reflect, we can solve problems, we can pass on our knowledge from generation to generation.

For example, mankind can write poems, invent fire and build civilizations. Reflection on knowledge gained is the beauty of human life; it is the one trait that seemingly has enabled us to go beyond our physical limitations and allowed us to survive as a species.

Being moral implies that we wisely use our thinking ability. Being moral means that we will not do anything that needlessly destroys or diminishes our rational nature. For example, taking drugs just to "blow our minds" is somehow inhuman; it does not fit what we define as a person. It is, therefore, wrong. We must bring cold hard reason to moral problems; it is one of the greatest gifts given to humans to do right.

• *We are free.* Without freedom, there is no right and wrong. Doing right or choosing wrong implies that we are free enough to choose. As we saw in Chapter 1, not everyone agrees that humans are free beings. For example, B. F. Skinner, a modern psychologist, believes that all human behavior is learned. He thinks that we are conditioned to act the way we do by the environment. Experience proves Skinner wrong.

It is true that a lot of what we are is determined by heredity and environment. It is also true, however, that we have a certain degree of freedom to change what we are, to improve what we are, to do new things.

For example, when you finish reading this chapter you could—if you want to—go and say something nice to a friend. You do not have to; no one is forcing you to do so. But if you do—or if you don't—it is something you freely choose to do or not do. To be moral is to use your freedom wisely, to use it in a human way.

• *We can love.* What is more human than to love? Loving is using our freedom in such a way as to do good for others. It is the greatest ability men and women have, the greatest aspect of what we are as humans. When Jesus tells us to love others as we love ourselves he is merely telling us to be human. Murder, rape, theft, and lying are wrong because they are failures to love; they are a misuse of freedom. On the other hand, a parent sacrificing for a child, a friend buying a gift for a loved one, a person giving up his or her life for another—all these are moral acts because they are preeminently human acts, loving acts. To do the right thing is to do the loving thing.

• *We have bodies.* Thought, freedom and love are part of mankind's spiritual nature. These traits comprise the functions of the so-called soul of human life. But humans are body-people, too. We are very much a part of the created universe. As the famous poem "Desiderata" puts it: "You are a child of the universe." As a child of the universe, you share in its material reality. You have a body. It is immoral not to care for that body. Why? Well, for one thing, you cannot think clearly, exercise your freedom or love if you have not taken proper care of your body. It is indeed a sacred part of you.

For example, we sense that people are acting inhumanly when they "get bombed out of their heads." We say that they act like animals. It is behavior unbecoming a human. The moral thing is to care for and respect our material nature. The fact that God himself became man (the Incarnation) in the person of his Son, Jesus Christ, further stresses the sacredness of bodily existence. By becoming one of us, Our Lord made us and our whole existence holy. The fact that his Spirit dwells in us—his temples—drives home the point that our bodies are sacred and are to be cherished with the deepest respect.

2. We are related to others in community.

• *We are beings with and for others.* More than any other species on this planet, humans need one another. We come into being through the love of two other people. We survive the trials of infancy and childhood through the care and concern of other people: parents, brothers and sisters, teachers, friends and the like. We thrive in adulthood by relating to others in the work world, by having families, by nourishing friendships. We need other people.

The other side of the coin is that other people need us. Our talents and abilities help others survive, too. To others, we give friendships, love, service, a trade and many innumerable other things as well. We cannot be human and escape others.

To be moral is to be with and for others because this is what it means to be human. To be antipeople is to be immoral, in-human. For example, we condemn suicide for many reasons but mainly because it is the prime example of an antisocial act. A person who takes his or her own life has given up on others, has cut all ties with others. This is not a human thing to do and is thus immoral.

- *We are beings with a history.* By being a member of the human community we have a history, we have roots. We inherit all the benefits (and mistakes, as well) of those who have gone before us. It is inhuman and immoral to destroy heedlessly that which has been given to us.

Likewise, we are in a process of history. Some will come after us. The human, moral thing to do is to recognize that what we do today has consequences for tomorrow. Caring about the depletion of the world's resources is right because it recognizes that we have obligations to tomorrow's generations, it affirms our human nature of caring about the history of others who are to make their home on this globe with us.

DIVINE REVELATION UNVEILS OUR TRUE IDENTITY. Christians believe that our God has entered human history. We believe that he has made a covenant of love with his people. This story of God's revelation, his love, is found in the Bible. The Old Testament story prepares the way for God's own entry onto the human scene in the person of his Son, Jesus Christ. We Christians firmly believe that by imitating the most human of humans, Jesus, and by listening to what he and his Father have said about us, we can find our true identity.

- *We are images of God.* To be an image of God is to be a reflection of him. What we believe is that human life is a reflection of divine life.

> God created man in his image;
>   in the divine image he created him;
>   male and female he created them (Gn 1:27).

Precisely in our ability to think and to love freely we mirror the very life of God. Each of us is a word of God, uttered in his own mysterious way, never to be repeated. Christian belief holds that you are unique, you are God's own image in the world. As a result, each of us is priceless. We are valuable. We are worth loving. We are worth dying for, as Jesus demonstrated to us on the Cross. To deny our uniqueness, our talents, our fundamental goodness is to act immorally, inhumanly. To use our talents, to appreciate the person that we are, to use our God-given minds and our freedom to love is to act godlike and to be moral. "The glory of God is man fully alive." All human life is of incalculable worth, its source is in God the Father. Morality has to do with recognizing this sublime truth and then living this truth in the attitudes and actions of our daily lives.

• *We are stewards of the Father.* A steward is one who watches over something; he or she is a partner in God's creative plan. Genesis puts it well: "Be fertile and multiply; fill the earth and subdue it. Have dominion over the fish of the sea, the birds of the air, and all the living things that move on the earth" (Gn 1:28). To have dominion over all of created reality is an awesome responsibility. It is a gift which we must use wisely. In bringing children into the world, in using (not abusing) the goods of the earth, in developing the material things left for us, humans must act with foresight and prudence. Not to do so is immoral.

• *We are God's children and his friends.* The Christian believes that the most profound reality about the human person is that we are God's children, that he cares for us, that our final destiny is union with him. Read the following verse meditatively:

> Can a mother forget her infant,
>   be without tenderness for the
>   child of her womb?
> Even should she forget,
>   I will never forget you.
>
> See, upon the palms of my hands
>   I have written your name. . .
>   (Is 49:15-16).

What a profound dignity we have as humans.

> See what love the Father has
>   bestowed on us
> in letting us be called the children of
>   God! (1 Jn 3:1)

Jesus has said, "I call you friends" (Jn 15:15). This gives each human person a unique worth and inalienable rights. As a result, no person should ever be treated as a thing, a means to an end. To be moral is to treat our fellow humans as brothers and sisters of our Lord and children of the Father. Much of Christian morality is summed up in this: Act towards others as though you were brothers and sisters!

• *As a result, humans are fundamentally good. However, we are also sinners.* The Christian brings a fundamental realism to what a human being is. We assert that a human is fundamentally good, not some depraved creature as William Golding suggested in the novel *The Lord of the Flies.* Our basic goodness is not something which we earned but is derived from the way God made us. Read the words of Genesis: "God looked at everything he had made, and he found it very good" (Gn 1:31).

However, Christians admit that our story is often a sad one of turning away from God's love. We sin. We do evil. We avoid the good. Hitler's killing of six million Jews and seven million other people he termed undesirable, the atomic bombs dropped on Hiroshima and Nagasaki, racial prejudice in America, religious discrimination in Northern Ireland, rich people glutting themselves while poor people starve—all are examples of the cruelty that people perpetrate on their brothers and sisters. We are undoubtedly beings of incredible cruelty when we want to be. However, this should never let us forget our true identity as a people redeemed by Jesus Christ who has rescued us from sin and death. Our tendency to do evil should not cloud our true identity as beings of incomparable worth and goodness found lovable by God with a destiny of union with him. As St. Augustine said in his *Confessions* (I, 1), "You have made us for yourself, O Lord, and our hearts are restless until they rest in you."

Conclusion: In summary, then, in trying to figure out the solution to moral problems, we should always ask the following: Is what I propose to do a human thing? Does this act tend to reveal what human life is really about or does it limit it? Is it thoughtful, an exercise of our freedom in love? Does it respect the fact that we are in community and responsible to the past as well as to the future? Does it cherish the uniqueness and worth of the individual person who is a body-person endowed with inalienable rights? Is it a responsible act of a child of God who has the divine command to care for created reality? Is it something a friend of Jesus would do, one who recognizes that he or she is an image of God fundamentally good and with an eternal destiny of union with him? If you can answer yes to these questions then what you propose to do is probably moral.

Discussion and an Exercise:

1. Consider the lifeboat case. Is what the captain did the human thing to do? Discuss some of these questions:

   a. Was anyone used as a means to an end?

   b. What was the captain's attitude to life?

   c. What might have been his idea of what human beings are?

2. Consider the drug case. In light of what you read in this section, advise Tom on what he should do.

3. Check any items from the list below which would qualify as immoral acts because they are essentially inhuman acts.

   ———— Engaging prisoners in medical experiments with cancer-causing drugs without their prior knowledge

   ———— Manned space explorations

   ———— Reading pornographic literature

   ———— Selling pornographic literature

   ———— Smoking in public places

———— Living alone on a desert island

———— Becoming a hermit to pray

———— Voting into power a communist government

———— In a democracy, refusing to vote

———— Not studying

———— Having a musical ability and not developing it

———— Driving a motorcycle without a helmet

———— Downgrading oneself constantly

———— Refusing to help at the scene of an accident

a. What do you think is inhuman about the action in the items you have checked?

b. For which items would you like to know more facts, circumstances, intentions and the like? Explain why.

IMAGINATION

You have probably noticed in working through the STOP sign that there has been a heavy emphasis on using your intellect, your rational ability in solving moral problems. There is a good reason for this: people often do not like to think, to reason things out. They often jump to conclusions based on emotion or take intellectual shortcuts. Escaping from thinking is one of the diseases associated with the inability to solve moral issues.

These escapes take many forms. Some people simply obey what others tell them to do without ever examining the reasons for the rules. Others imitate their "heroes" and their behavior without carefully considering if that behavior is good or bad. Still others simply say that all morality is just a matter of taste. They claim that there is no right and wrong that people can agree on. This is a form of intellectual laziness. Finally, others follow the crowd and pick up its values without critically thinking through the implications of them. Conformity is the key word for this group of non-thinkers.

The STOP sign is designed to make a person dig out the facts and reflect on them before making a decision. But good, hard rational thought is not the only mental process that separates human life from that of the animals. Creative imagination is also a very valuable human attribute that can be a powerful guide in distinguishing right from wrong. Hard thought often comes before the breakthroughs discovered by one's imagination.

Take Christopher Columbus, for example. His genius of imagining a round world was preceded by years of exploration and sailing, of watching the stars and charting the currents. He was ready for a discovery because he had prepared for it. Likewise with Isaac Newton. Most people had seen apples fall from trees before. But Newton was ready to see the principle of gravity because he had mentally prepared for it.

The discovery of the cure for polio was an imaginative breakthrough which came after years of basic research and testing. We would do well to remember Thomas Edison's famous quote: "Genius is one percent inspiration and ninety-nine percent perspiration."

Creative imagination following good, hard thought has a role to play in morality, too. Mohandas Gandhi is sometimes considered one of the great political and moral leaders of this century. Why? He was a man of imagination. He saw that violence was not the only way to throw off British rule in India. He taught that passive resistance could bring about the desired end of freedom without the shedding of blood. His ideas caught on and the result was independence for the nation of India.

Another example of a creative moral thinker was Martin Luther King. His "dream" (imaginative thinkers are often dreamers) was that blacks in this country could be treated fairly and equally. He preached his dream and convinced enough of his countrymen that the dream could become real without massive bloodshed.

A final example is Jesus himself. He had the most creative

imagination of anyone. He looked at a leper and saw his brother; he looked at a prostitute and saw his sister. Jesus could even say to his enemies, "I forgive you." It takes imagination to say that. Jesus' dream of people treating one another as they would like to be treated upset the conventional wisdom of his day and started a religion whose influence will never end.

What does all this mean for you? It means this: bring your imagination to the problem at this point in your study. Try to dream a little. See if you cannot think of new approaches in light of the facts and data you have unearthed. Consider new alternatives, new approaches to your problem. What may seem far-fetched may very well be the breakthrough you have been waiting for. A marvelous quote from the famous play *Man of La Mancha* might be helpful here. Miguel de Cervantes is defending his hero Don Quixote and his imaginative dreaming:

> When life itself seems lunatic, who knows where madness lies? Perhaps to be too practical is madness. To surrender dreams—this may be madness. To seek treasure where there is only trash. Too much sanity may be madness. And maddest of all, to see life as it is and not as it should be.[2]

---

[2] Dale Wasserman, Joe Darion and Mitch Leigh, *Man of La Mancha* (New York. Dell Publishing Co., Inc., 1966), p. 99.

For Discussion and Analysis:

1. Having discussed the lifeboat case thus far, can you imaginatively come up with any new insights? Discuss them.

2. Can you think of any new approaches to the drug case in light of what you have already discussed?

3. Discuss the following case. This time try to be as imaginative as possible. Run it through the STOP sign; emphasize in your analysis some creative alternatives.

Case: "Teaching the Teacher"

> For a period of a month, you have been on the receiving end of verbal abuse from a certain teacher. In addition, you are clearly convinced that the teacher has been grading your essay exams unfairly. After one conference with the teacher, you are pretty sure he is prejudiced against you because of an older brother whom the teacher had in class several years ago. Your brother was known to be an unruly student.

> You are contemplating "getting even" with the teacher. Your friends suggest that you might slash his tires in order to teach him a lesson.

> What would you do?

Discussion:

1. What issues are involved in this situation?

2. Are there other ways to deal with an unjust "authority figure"? Explain.

3. If you slash the tires, what might result?

4. What values will you be bringing to the solution of this case?

5. How might your friends help you solve the situation?

LAW (Principles—Authority)

Law, ethical and moral principles, and authority are all help-ful guides in doing the right thing. (For the sake of discussion, principles and authority will be treated here under the heading of law.) The problem with law as a guide to doing right, however, is that for many people it is seen as a bad thing. People remember only too clearly the cry of certain politicians for "law and order" and yet these same politicians were guilty of lying, gross theft and political crimes committed against the very people who voted them into power. This is an example of hypocrisy; the usefulness of law as a guide to doing right should not be judged by lawbreakers.

At its best, law represents the accumulated wisdom of those who have gone before us. It represents an objective norm of morality against which we can measure our behavior. We have some degree of light in the solution of most of our moral problems because we have law to guide us, to show us the right thing to do. Very often we can look to the law as the proper way to solve our problems.

Some people claim that law makes us less free and thus is bad. This might be true of bad law, but not of good law. Good law aids and protects freedom, it does not limit it. Freedom does not mean license. License is doing whatever you want whenever you want. With license, freedom is destroyed. For example, if you were allowed to shoot off a gun wherever and whenever you wanted to, you would destroy the freedom of others. With no traffic laws, none of us would be free to drive in safety. With no tax laws, none of us would enjoy the many benefits and freedoms that living in a society can give to us.

What constitutes good law? St. Thomas Aquinas gave the best definition of law. His definition attributes the following char-acteristics to law: (1) it is reasonable; (2) it is directed to the common good; (3) it is made by competent authority; and (4) it must be properly promulgated. Let us briefly examine each of these elements.

1. *Law is reasonable.* If law is to be a guide to doing right it must be reasonable. It makes eminent sense for operators of cars to drive on the same side of the street when going in a given direction. This is reasonable because the purpose of the law is to prevent the loss of life. However, imagine the following law: "All drivers of automobiles must drive blindfolded"! This law is totally irrational; it is a bad law. It is absolutely no guide to doing the right thing.

2. *Law is for the common good.* What this means is that good law helps build up a society, it is for the good of the individuals within it. Making wage earners pay taxes is a good law if the money used from the taxes will benefit society, for example, by providing police protection, schools, orphanages and the like. However, laws which discriminate against the hiring of women would be bad laws. Discrimination destroys the common good; it brings about tension and violence in society. It excludes many who could help to build the society.

3. *Law must be made by competent authority.* If someone came up to you and told you that you must always write with your left hand you would probably laugh at the person. For one thing, it is a dumb rule, it is unreasonable. For another, the person telling you to write lefthanded has no authority to tell you to do so. However, if a lifeguard instructs you not to bring glass bottles onto the deck of the swimming pool because of the possibility of broken glass and resultant injuries, you would probably listen to him. His rule is reasonable and directed to the safety of people; moreover, he has the authority by virtue of his position to tell you what to do. In a similar vein, laws passed by our Congress are laws written by competent authority. In our system of government, members of Congress are elected by the people. We have delegated authority to them and have agreed to listen to the laws they enact. They are a proper governing body.

4. *Law must be promulgated.* Promulgation means that a law is advertised, that people can reasonably be expected to know it. Imagine the outcry in high schools if tomorrow teachers gave

detentions to all boys who did not wear a flattop haircut and to all girls who did not wear two pigtails. You would not only laugh hysterically at the absurdity of the rule, you would scream against the unfairness of it. How can you be held accountable for a law which you did not even know about?

Law has traditionally been treated under four categories: natural law, civil law, divine law and church law. All these are excellent guides in doing the right thing. The following presents a brief description of each.

Natural Law. Most normal and reasonable people are appalled at the thought of parents brutally beating their children. Why? Simply put, because it is unnatural. God's plan is for parents to care for and protect their young. To victimize innocent and defenseless children mercilessly is gross, absurd and sick. It goes against the way things are meant to be. Natural law refers to our ability to understand what it means to be human and what must be done to develop as humans; it refers to those principles held to be derived from nature and binding upon human society. Natural law can be discovered by reasonable people. God has made creation a certain way and he provided men and women with minds to discover the way things are.

The Ten Commandments are a real reflection of the natural law because their purpose is to describe a positive form of human loving. They help guide us to a *reasonable* approach to living our lives in harmony with the "way things are." The result of following God's plan in creation (natural law) is happiness; upsetting that plan most often brings unhappiness.

Civil law. Civil law is *human* law made for the smooth functioning of the particular groups to which we belong. Often, civil law is a particular application of the natural law. For example, it seems that the natural law forbids humans from indiscriminately killing each other. Why? Well, it stands to reason that if killing at will were allowed, there could be no society. Moreover, there could not even be a family unit if, for example, a father decided that he could do away with his children whenever they got in the way. Humanity would dissolve. Particular societies have taken this law of nature (that is, "Don't kill humans indiscriminately") and have made particular laws for their own situation. Thus, we drive on the right side of the road in America. In England, they drive on the left side. The purpose of both laws is the same: namely, to protect the indiscriminate killing of human life.

Civil law is an excellent guide to doing the right thing in a particular society if you want to be a member of that society. The one problem with civil law, however, is that because it is human law, it is not always good law. For example, laws permitting abortion on demand are, from our faith perspective, bad laws. There is no moral obligation to obey bad law. We should try to change it. At times, we may have to disobey it. For example, Hitler's laws directed against the Jews were bad, immoral civil laws. Today, we admire as heroes those who refused to obey the discrimination against and killing of the Jews.

Divine law. Divine law is given to us by God himself. St. Thomas listed four reasons why God has given humans the help of divine law: (1) It helps us achieve our eternal destiny of union with him. (2) Because humans can come up with different answers on what they should do, God has given help on what we should do and what we should avoid. (3) God's law helps get at the motivations, the intentions of what we do; human law can only get at the external acts themselves. (4) Divine law helps point out sin, the failure to grow in a living, loving relationship with God and others.

Divine law ultimately resides in God himself and in his Word, Jesus Christ. The Ten Commandments are the best summary of divine law found in the Old Testament; the Beatitudes found in the New Testament are an excellent summary of how Christians should respond to God and to neighbor. These Commandments are not what some people humorously refer to as suggestions. Jesus himself said that "If you love me, keep my Commandments." All of the Commandments deal with concrete ways of loving, of responding to both God and neighbor. Each of them tries to get at some basic value, a value which is at the root of human happiness. Certainly, for the Jews of the Old Testament and the disciples of Jesus, they were not seen as burdensome lists to be obeyed. Rather, they help give the good person a sense of identity. By living the Commandments and the Beatitudes, Christians are responding to their call as God's special people who love in a special way. Below is a list of the Commandments and the Beatitudes with a brief description of the values which are preserved in the Commandment or the Beatitude. Please study the list carefully.

THE TEN COMMANDMENTS
(Dt 5:6-21; Ex 20:2-17)

Commandment   **Values**

"Loving God above all things"

1. I, the Lord, am your God. You shall not have other gods besides me.
   - making God the goal of our life
   - refusing to substitute things such as sex, money, power or prestige for our true purpose in life

2. You shall not take the name of the Lord, your God, in vain.
   - respecting God's name
   - care in the way we worship and humility in prayer
   - appreciating the sacredness of God and things associated with him

3. Remember to keep holy the Sabbath.
   - properly worshipping God
   - giving centrality to the day of the Lord, the day of Jesus' resurrection
   - appreciation for the fact that we approach God in community; our salvation is realized with others

"Loving your neighbor as yourself"

4. Honor your father and your mother.
   - parents should reflect God's love by respecting, caring for and loving their children

	• children respecting their parents and proper authority through obedience, respect and courtesy. • family members, brothers and sisters for example, living as a community of love
5. You shall not kill.	• respect for God's greatest gift, life • includes: respect for our bodies, avoiding harmful substances, getting rest and relaxation • includes: respect for the "least of these"—the unborn, the old, the sick and dying
6. You shall not commit adultery.	• respect and appreciation for our sexual nature • sees sex as a share in God's creative plan, used with respect, care and love within marriage • the virtue of chastity—sex within the context of love
7. You shall not steal.	• the virtue of trust extolled; avoids stealing, cheating, shoplifting • using God-given talents and gifts to our ability
8. You shall not bear false witness against your neighbor.	• the virtue of honesty • respects the good name, reputation and life-style of others
9. You shall not covet your neighbor's wife.	• right attitudes as well as right action; pure intention
10. You shall not covet anything that belongs to your neighbor	• avoiding an attitude of "I must have" • avoiding jealousy

THE BEATITUDES (Mt 5:3-10)

Beatitude	Values
1. How blest are the poor in spirit; the reign of God is theirs.	• putting trust in God, not things
2. Blest too are the sorrowing: they shall be consoled.	• patient suffering and enduring hardships reap their reward
3. Blest are the lowly; they shall inherit the land.	• humility in all we do; nonviolence
4. Blest are they who hunger and thirst for holiness; they shall have their fill.	• getting involved helping the downtrodden; working for the equality of people
5. Blest are they who show mercy; mercy shall be theirs.	• mercy and forgiveness
6. Blest are the single-hearted; for they shall see God.	• "loving God with one's whole heart, whole mind, whole soul"
7. Blest are the peacemakers; they shall be called sons of God.	• peacemaking; loving those who are hard to love
8. Blest are those persecuted for holiness' sake; the reign of God is theirs.	• being willing to suffer for the right thing, even if abused verbally or physically; accepting the consequences of living a good life

Church law. What civil law is to natural law, church law is to divine law. Belonging to a particular society brings with it certain obligations. So, too, belonging to a particular faith community brings with it certain duties. For example, divine law holds that we should worship God. Church law says that in our particular faith community we will worship together on the Lord's day in remembrance of what Jesus accomplished for us on Calvary and his victory over death on Easter Sunday. Church law will be discussed at greater length in the next chapter.

Exercises:

1. One of the bestselling books of the '70s was entitled *The Book of Lists*. In the spirit of that book, below please find a list of laws which exist, have existed or may very well exist by the year 2000. Check those laws which you think are clearly examples of bad laws.

     1. All youngsters must take a pill that will enable them to learn at three times the normal rate.

     2. The speed limit for expressways is 55 mph.

     3. Retarded children should be put to death.

     4. Because of its connection with cancer, the growing, selling or smoking of any kind of tobacco is prohibited.

     5. Anyone refusing to fight in defense of his or her country will be summarily executed.

     6. No one should eat in public.

     7. Motorcyclists must wear safety helmets.

     8. There will be no capital punishment.

     9. Littering is punishable by a year's imprisonment.

     10. Everyone must worship in the church of one's choice once a week.

     11. Interracial marriage is forbidden.

     12. Factories must install pollution control devices to meet certain air quality standards.

     13. Jaywalking is prohibited.

     14. Movies of the X-rated variety shall not be produced.

       a. Why did you check the items you did? How do they violate one or more of the conditions of good law as described by St. Thomas?

    b. For the items you did not check, how could you defend them as being good laws?

2. Consider the lifeboat case. Apply what you learned in this section of the chapter to this case. Was there any civil law to prevent what the captain did? Any natural or divine law?

3. Discuss how law might have helped Tom make a decision in the drug case described at the end of the last chapter.

SUMMARY:

1. This chapter began a discussion of the elements around the STOP sign. Christians should consult the teaching of Jesus, who is our norm in moral decision-making. Two questions that must be asked are:

    a. Is this a loving action?

    b. Is this a serving action?

2. Morality has to do with the human. Reason and revelation are great aids in discovering what constitutes what human acts are. Reason indicates that we are spiritual-material beings who can think, love in freedom and have bodies. It also tells us that we are in community with others, being with and for them. We are also beings with a history.

3. Divine revelation unveils our true identity as images of God, stewards of the Father, God's children and friends, fundamentally good, though sinners.

4. Balanced with good, hard thought, creative imagination may often give us insight into the solution of moral problems.

5. Law is the objective norm of morality. Good law is reasonable, promotes the common good, is given by proper authority and promulgated. The kinds of law commonly discussed are:

a. Natural law—the way things are, based on how God made them.

b. Civil law—the particular application of natural law in given societies.

c. Divine law—given to us by God to help us in our journey toward him. The Ten Commandments and the Beatitudes are excellent summaries of divine law.

d. Church law—the particular application of divine law to the Christian community.

A FINAL CASE—"Windfall"

You have just returned from a record store where you purchased a recent recording of a favorite group. Much to your surprise you discover that the clerk gave $10 too much in change. (You had paid for the record with a $10 bill; apparently, the clerk thought you had given her $20.)

Would you keep the money?

Discussion:

1. In light of the past two chapters, explain your decision.

2. Would it be dishonest to keep the money?

3. Does the amount make any difference in your decision? What if she had given you a $100 bill? a $1 bill?

4. Have the profits the store makes from your regular shopping there entitled you to this bonus? If you said "yes" are you rationalizing, that is, just making an excuse for your behavior? Or is this a legitimate reason to keep the money? Explain.

4

The STOP Sign, Concluded

Conscience is the true vicar of Christ in the soul; a proph-
et in its information; a monarch in its preemptoriness;
a priest in its blessings or anathemas, according as we
obey or disobey it.
—John Henry Cardinal Newman

This present chapter will conclude our discussion of the process of moral decision-making known as the STOP sign. The elements treated in the chapter include: the church as a source of
moral guidance, values, instinct and conscience.

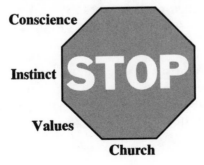

Conscience

Instinct

Values

Church

CHURCH

For the Catholic, the church provides a rich source of guidance in the making of moral decisions. Catholics believe that Jesus remains active in his church, his body, by virtue of a strong promise made by him. In addition, we believe that he handed on his teaching authority to the disciples and their successors. The last words of Jesus in Matthew's Gospel give the church the confidence to teach in his name:

> Full authority has been given to me
> both in heaven and on earth;
> go, therefore, and make disciples of all the nations.
> Baptize them in the name
> of the Father,
> and of the Son,
> and of the Holy Spirit.
> Teach them to carry out everything I have
> commanded you.
> And know that I am with you always, until
> the end of the world! (Mt 28: 18-20)

Thus, the first reason it is very worthwhile to listen to the teaching of the church in moral matters is that Jesus remains active in the church, guiding it and its members to him and his Father. The second reason is the very real help a faith community can be in supporting the individuals in the church family. St. Paul alludes to this when he refers to the church as the body of Christ:

> You, then, are the body of Christ. Every one of
> you is a member of it. Furthermore, God has set
> up in the church first apostles, second prophets,
> third teachers, then miracle workers, healers, assis-
> tants, administrators, and those who speak in
> tongues (1 Cor 12:27-28).

As members of Christ's body, we all have different roles, different functions, the purpose of which is to build up the body, to help the other members in it. All of us have a special value in the church because of the potential aid we can be to the other members.

The question remains, then, to whom do we turn for guidance in the church when we are trying to do the right thing? There are at least three groups of people to whom we can look for guidance: the teachers in the church, our religious guides and our fellow believers.

Teachers in the Church

The primary teacher in the church is the pope. Teaching in conjunction with the pope are the bishops, the successors to the apostles. Their teaching in moral matters can be found in a number of places. Preeminent among these sources are the documents of ecumenical councils of the church. The most recent ecumenical council was Vatican II, held in the early 1960s. That particular council produced a number of documents which touched on concerns of the moral life. One of the most important of the documents was entitled *Pastoral Constitution on the Church in the Modern World*. Among other topics, this document reaffirmed the dignity of the human person and restated the church's condemnation of abortion and euthanasia.

Another important source of moral teaching is papal encyclicals. Encyclicals are letters sent to the worldwide church addressing certain topics. Two of the most important ones written by Pope Paul VI were *Humanae Vitae (Of Human Life)* and *Populorum Progressio (On the Development of Peoples)*. The former deals with topics in the area of life and love, especially birth control and family planning; the latter concerns itself with themes in the areas of world poverty and social justice.

Popes often give moral teaching in speeches, too. An extremely important one by Pope Pius XII on the topic of euthanasia is cited in the appendix to Chapter 8. In addition, bishops often send out pastoral letters to the people of their dioceses on issues of moral concern. An important recent pastoral letter was composed by the American bishops in 1976 and addressed moral topics of concern to the family, the nation and the community of nations. Its title is *To Live in Christ Jesus*.

Religious Guides

Ordinarily, but unfortunately, the average Catholic does not read the documents of the councils, nor the encyclicals and pastoral letters of the pope and bishops. This is where our religious guides have an important role to play in helping to solve moral problems. Religious guides include our parish priests, our confessor, theologians and the religious press.

The teaching found in church documents often filters down to the "person in the pew" through the preaching done by our priests. Obviously, for a concerned person, a 15-minute Sunday homily will not satisfy his or her curiosity about church moral teaching. As a result, consultation with a favorite confessor can be a good way of receiving church teaching about moral issues, and an opportunity to discuss in depth the moral problems one is having. Also, reading periodicals or the books of moral theologians can be of great help. On a weekly basis, the local diocesan newspaper usually treats some area of church moral teaching. Magazines such as *U.S. Catholic, Sign, St. Anthony Messenger, America, Liguorian* and the like present readable accounts of what is going on in the moral teaching of the church. Also, there are a number of topflight Roman Catholic theologians who are in the forefront, examining moral issues. Reading them and following their line of argumentation usually take a bit of work, but the effort is always worthwhile because of the intellectual stimulation they provide. Anyone serious about finding out what the church has to say on a particular issue will make the effort to consult some of these sources.

Fellow Believers

Another source of guidance in moral decision-making is our fellow believers. They can be of considerable help in working through moral problems. They not only share experiences with us, but they can often give us the necessary support to make a difficult decision to do the right thing. It is so difficult to go against the crowd in our contemporary society; at times, we might feel very much alone in taking an unpopular stand. Our fellow believers form a community of strength and faith which can sustain us in doing right against all the pressures modern society puts on us. We would be foolish not to seek out and ask the advice of those fellow Christians we admire for their holiness, their balance, their basic goodness. It is true that they cannot make the decision for us, but they can give us encouragement, help and prayer.

A final word should be said about canon law, or church law. As we saw in the last chapter, church law is designed for the smooth functioning of the church community. Just as civil law is necessary for those living in a given society, so, too, church law is necessary to guide church members in their day-to-day living of Christian community. The most important church laws for the Catholic are described below:

1. To keep holy the day of the Lord's resurrection: to worship God by participating in Mass every Sunday and Holy Days of Obligation; to avoid those activities that would hinder renewal of soul and body, e.g., needless work and business activities, unnecessary shopping, etc.

2. To lead a sacramental life: to receive Holy Communion frequently and the sacrament of Penance regularly; minimally, to receive the sacrament of Reconciliation at least once a year (annual confession is obligatory only if serious sin is involved).
   —minimally, to receive Holy Communion at least once a year, between the First Sunday of Lent and Trinity Sunday.

3. To study Catholic teaching in preparation for the sacrament of Confirmation, to be confirmed, and then to study and advance the cause of Christ.

4. To observe the marriage laws of the church; to give religious training (by example and word) to one's children; to use parish schools and religious education programs.

5. To strengthen and support the church: one's own parish community and parish priests; the worldwide church and the pope.

6. To do penance, including abstaining from meat and fasting from food on appointed days.

7. To join in the missionary spirit and apostolate of the church.

(Taken from *Basic Teachings for Catholic Religious Education.* U. S. Catholic Conference, 1973, p. 28.)

Exercises:

1. Discuss both the lifeboat case and the drug case with at least three fellow believers. Did they come up with any insights you did not think of? Share your conversations with your classmates.

2. Study the laws of the church as listed above. Discuss whether each qualifies as a good law according to the criteria of Thomas Aquinas:

   a. reasonable,

   b. for the common good,

   c. given by proper authority,

   d. promulgated.

3. Research at least one article from a popular Catholic periodical on a moral issue. Report your findings to the class.

VALUES

Many problems in the area of morality involve a conflict of values. For example, the woman who is contemplating an abortion is really in conflict over at least two values: the value of her own reputation or mental/physical health versus the value of the life of the baby. When a person is contemplating cheating on an exam, there is a conflict over the value of honesty versus the value of obtaining a high grade on the exam. Schools which are thinking about setting up a system for admitting more members of minority groups are involved in weighing the value of treating everyone on an equal basis versus the value of righting centuries of wrongdoing and the neglect of minority groups. As a final example, the father who wants to do volunteer work for two years in some foreign country must weigh the value of caring for and raising his immediate family versus the value of helping the poor and less fortunate in another area of the world.

Before making a moral decision, it is advisable to separate the values which are involved in the issue. Secondly, it is important to clarify which of the values involved is most important to you as you try to work through the decision. By definition, values result from a process of valuing. Professors Raths, Harmin and Simon describe this process quite well in their classic book entitled *Values and Teaching*. They claim something is a value to you if you (1) choose it, (2) prize it, and (3) act on it. "Choosing" implies that you do it freely, from among alternatives, and after thoughtfully considering the consequences of each alternative. "Prizing" means that you cherish your choice, are happy with it and are willing to say so publicly. "Acting on your choice" affirms that you do something with it, and do so repeatedly, so that there is a definite pattern in your life.

Take the example of the person who says that he values life. He may very well say it, but in reality he drives like a madman, risking his life and those of others. If he does not act on what he says is his value, then it is clearly not a value. One of the most disgusting examples of someone who claims he values something but does not act on it is the politician who cries "law and order" on the one hand, but steals from the public on the other. Law and order may be OK, but for others, not for himself. In contrast to this example is a person who declares that religion is a value in his or her life. Such a person will pray, will be willing to speak out in defense of religious values, even if it is unpopular to do so, and will live a style of life that is consistent with his or her professed beliefs.

Why is it important to examine and clarify your values in making moral decisions? For one reason, it helps simplify the issue. Knowing precisely what is involved in the choice may make the decision easier. Consider the case of the father who is offered a job in another city at higher pay. He really contemplates taking the job but it will entail more travel and more time away from the family. The decision is not an easy one. In clarifying his values, he might discover that it is a case of more money versus time with his family. If he highly values his family (and it may be difficult for him to decide if this is so), he will probably tend to turn down the job, regardless of the greater salary. The decision will be difficult; but, at least, he will know what he is choosing and why he is choosing it.

A second reason for clarifying the values involved in the particular case is because it will tend to show which values are more important than others. For example, human life is a value. A good reputation is a value, too. But human life is more important than a good reputation. The teenage girl who is contemplating an abortion to save her reputation is in a real moral crisis. There is a definite conflict of values: the life of the baby versus her good reputation. Both are important. But regardless of the personal shame involved for the girl, we believe that human life is of greater value than a good reputation. Human life also outranks property. Both are values, but they are certainly not of equal merit. The mother who runs into a burning house to save her child may run right past her own room which contains an extremely valuable piece of jewelry. She almost instinctively goes for the baby because she knows that property can be replaced, but human life cannot be.

A third benefit that might result from clarifying the values involved in a moral decision is that one might be able to think of a way to preserve both values by arriving at a compromise decision. Take the teacher who is having trouble keeping order in her class. As a teacher, she might well value authority which translates into strict obedience of the rules that she has established and silence in the classroom. The students, on the other side, value their freedom, freedom to speak out, freedom to "visit" with their classmates, and the like. By clarifying both sides of the issue, namely, freedom and authority, perhaps a compromise can be established. Maybe the teacher and students will agree on a more democratic way of running the class which allows for both freedom and authority. In this case, both values can be preserved.

In conclusion, for this section of the STOP sign it is important to analyze the following steps:

1. Identify the values which are in conflict in the case.

2. If possible, rank the values.

3. See if you can preserve all the values by some compromise.

4. If compromise is impossible, clarify what is the most important value for you. In light of the rest of the decision-making process, choose the most important value.

Exercises:

It is necessary to apply what you read in this section by working through a number of different kinds of situations. Please try to work through all of these.

1. Take the drug case involving Tom and Jack. Here an identification of the values is rather simple: the value of not betraying a friend versus the value of human health and life. In light of this:

    a. Rank these two values. (Might there be other values involved as well? Might friendship and life be impossible to set against each other? If so, what else must be taken into consideration?)

   b. Is there a way to get Jack to stop dealing in
      drugs and yet not betray his friendship, that
      is, is it possible to preserve both values?

   c. Clarify which is the most important value for
      you. In light of what you have read in this
      book thus far, which value do you think in
      this case *ought* to be the most important to
      you? Explain your answer.

2. Consider the lifeboat case again. Ask these four
   questions:

   a. What are the conflicting values?

   b. How should these values be ranked?

   c. Is it possible to preserve all the values in-
      volved?

   d. Which is the most important value to you?
      Why?

3. Below are listed some Christian values of extreme
   importance. Find in the New Testament an example
   of how Jesus valued each of them:

   • justice

   • mercy

   • respect for the individual

   • peace

   • care for the lowly

   • trust in others

   • honesty

   • life

   a. What values were in conflict in the case of
      the woman caught in adultery? How did
      Jesus solve this moral dilemma?

   b. What values were in conflict in the ques-
      tion of whether a Jew should pay taxes to
      Caesar? How did Jesus resolve the conflict?

4. In the following list of brief cases, identify and rank the values in conflict:

   a. whether to shoot to kill looters in a race riot,

   b. whether to burn surplus crops to maintain an economy,

   c. whether to indulge in sexual relations outside of marriage,

   d. whether to ban pornographic books,

   e. whether a parent should spank a child to discipline him or her,

   f. whether a supersonic jet transport system should be built,

   g. whether taxes should be increased for more foreign aid,

   h. whether a minority quota system should be established for entrance to law schools,

   i. whether children should be bused to schools to obtain equal educational opportunities.

5. Clarify some of your own values. Check which of the following is most representative of what you think or would do.

   a. You have just won $100 in a church raffle. What would you most likely do with the money?

      ——— Give some of it to the poor.
      ——— Buy something for yourself.
      ——— Save it for school.

   b. Your best friend is hooked on drugs. What would you do?

      ——— Tell his or her parents.
      ——— Tell a school counselor.
      ——— Take him or her to a drug clinic.

   c. You are trying to decide what kind of job you'll take after graduation. Which of these is most appealing to you?

      ——— Teach retarded kids.
      ——— Become a business executive.
      ——— Work in a factory.

d. Imagine you are on a desert island for a year. Which of the following would you rather have with you?

—— a set of encyclopedias.
—— the bible.
—— the collected works of your favorite author.

e. If you thought you were going to die in a week, how would you spend your remaining days?

—— with your family.
—— with your friends.
—— traveling.

f. For which group of people do you feel most sorry?

—— the sick.
—— the lonely.
—— homosexuals.

g. A close friend has just painted a picture for you. You don't like it. When she asks for your opinion, what would you do?

—— Be honest.
—— Tell her you liked it.
—— Give it a little praise.

h. What do you fear the most?

—— being a failure at school.
—— not having many friends.
—— not making enough money.

i. How would you prefer your tax dollars be spent?

—— on the poor.
—— on cancer research.
—— on energy research.

6. Draw a coat of arms for your religious values. Draw a symbolic picture in each of the areas to depict your beliefs about each of the following questions.

   a. What do you think is the most serious moral issue in the world today?

   b. What virtue best describes you?

   c. What trait of Jesus do you most admire?

   d. What one value would you never surrender, even if threatened with death?

   e. What person do you most admire?

   f. What one quality in your life would you like to change for the better? If you want to, share it with others.

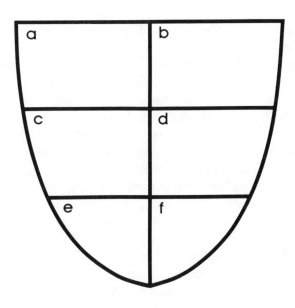

INSTINCT

Psychologists and others who study human behavior and thinking processes have observed that there are distinct hemispheres to the human brain. The left hemisphere controls most of our rational processes. It is most involved in reasoning and intellectualizing. Psychologists claim that for people in the Western world the left side of the brain is the dominant hemisphere. We tend to look at issues and problems basically from a rational point of view. The right side of the brain, on the other hand, is more concerned with intuition, creative insight, sensitive feeling. In most people in the Western world, it is not as prominent in their way of knowing. In other words, we have been trained to trust our reason but to distrust our intuition, our sensitive, almost instinctual approach to knowledge.

Many people today are calling for a balance between the two—a centering, if you will—which allows room for both cold, hard, rational analysis and sensitive intuitive insight to acquiring human knowledge. When this notion is applied to solving moral problems, what is being said here is that at times we almost have an "instinctual" sense of what is right or wrong in a certain situation. Our basic gut reaction, in other words, can often sense the harmony of a particular good action or the disharmony of a particular bad action. This is not to say, of course, that we should always trust our feelings, our gut reaction, our instinctive approach to a moral problem. We all know that feelings are powerful and, at times, blindingly wrong. However, what is meant is that maybe we should be a little more attentive to our feelings about a given situation. Another term for this is "moral imperative," that kind of response called for by the situation, your instinctual sense of right or wrong. A few examples may help.

Consider this moral case. Note your initial instinctual reaction even before you run through the STOP sign. By the way, your instinctual reaction is not necessarily your first one, "off the top of your head" or immediate. Rather, it flows from the depth of your moral personality and is a response of "yes" or "no." Suppose someone proposed that, when cloning humans becomes a reality, the government should only clone the brightest, best-looking white men and women. All other people would be sterilized so that they could not have children. This would easily be accomplished by introducing a sterilizing agent into the water supply. Cloning, of course, is asexual reproduction. A cell of a particular organism is reproduced to create an exact biological duplicate of the organism. Thus, if it could be done to humans, you could have an exact duplicate of Albert Einstein—or Adolf Hitler. In fact, you could have a thousand of them, a million or more. Now, how do you react to this? Most people would probably be appalled at the thought, without even thinking about it. Our instinctual reaction cries out against this: we feel it is wrong. That initial reaction has something to it. We should pay attention to it. It can be a good start for our moral reflection. Certainly, later we can check out the STOP sign and ask some good hard questions like: What does such a proposal do to the definition of sexual love? Marriage? Family life? Who will choose who shall be cloned? Why just white people? What will be the long-term effects? Is this a loving thing to do? Does it serve mankind? The answers to these and other questions will probably confirm very strongly what you felt instinctively about the proposal.

A second example is marvelously illustrated by an advertisement often run on television concerning environmental pollution. One version of the ad has an Indian who rides his horse to the top of a ridge and looks down on an air-polluted, littered highway. Another version has him canoeing on a filthy stream. In both, his reaction is the same: a gentle tear rolls down his cheek. A word is not spoken. That Indian does not have to be a sophisticated moralist, well-versed in all the other elements of the STOP sign. His "guts" tell him that what is going on is clearly wrong and immoral. Maybe on further reflection he could tell you why this is so, but note how his instinctual reaction gave him a clue to the immorality of pollution.

Professor Maguire points to a final example which concerns what some "experts" tell us about the need for more nuclear weaponry and an increase in the arms race. Their arguments sound so logical until we realize that we already possess the kill-power strong enough to wipe out each man, woman and child on this planet 100 times over. What is your instinctual reaction to their proposal? Should we commit more billions of dollars (which could be used for more fruitful purposes) so that we can step up our kill-power to 200 times for every man, woman and child? Perhaps your gut reaction screams no, and says enough is enough. Sure, you would be wise to study the issue further; but do not be easily convinced that the "experts" are correct on such an important issue.

A similar case, of course, involves abortion. People can use all the sophisticated arguments they want to about reasons to justify the abortion. But arguments like "it is only a mass of cells acting as a parasite on the mother" seem to quickly dissolve when you see a picture of a five-month-old aborted fetus: the little hands, the feet, the head. Your gut reaction might very well scream to you (and to others) that this is absurd. We are talking about human life. Let's "call a spade a spade" and at least admit that when we abort we take *human* life. Very few people can bear to look at pictures of aborted fetuses and come away with an easy conscience.

Your instinctual gut reactions to moral cases have a role to play in arriving at moral decisions. Pay attention to them, because they may help you decide to do the right thing. Certainly, check them out against the facts, against the teaching of Jesus, against the guidance offered by reason and revelation, by the church and the law. A sense of moral outrage evoked by our feelings can help us see the absurdity of many acts that either we or others propose to do. It will help us see clearly through a remark like that attributed to an American commander in Vietnam, who said that he had to destroy a village in order to save it. It can help put us on the right track before we rely too much on what others say.

CONSCIENCE

With a discussion of conscience, we have come full circle around the STOP sign. The moral decision-making process ends with this principle: *Follow your conscience*. After you have dug out the facts, prayed, reflected, listened to Jesus and the church, law and reason, and all the other elements around the STOP sign, you must eventually end up with a decision. Your decision must be a decision to act or not to act. (Incidentally, deciding not to decide is a kind of decision, a kind of action.) The best principle to follow at this point, then, is to follow your conscience. This very important principle comes after another important principle, which is to form your conscience and inform it continuously. The whole function of the STOP sign is to help you form your conscience. Using it or a similar method of learning about right and wrong is a great help in conscience formation. We are left, then, with only one question: "What is meant by conscience?"

What conscience is not. Before describing what conscience is, it might be helpful to say what it is not. First, it is not some kind of mechanical voice box telling me to do right or wrong. It is not a little guardian angel whispering in my ear directing me in my actions. It is not a feeling, whether the feeling be guilt, worry, dissatisfaction or restlessness.

What conscience is. There have been a number of attempts to describe the reality known as conscience. At the Second Vatican Council, the church fathers defined conscience as the most secret core and sanctuary of the human person. It is there that we are most alone with God whose voice echoes in our hearts. In this secret core of our being, we have a sense of right and wrong and a fundamental sense of responsibility. This sense of responsibility tells us that we are answerable for what we do. Before we act, it tells us what we ought to do. Secondly, it enables us to do something about this "ought." Thirdly, it looks back to judge whether what we did was right or wrong. Therefore, conscience comes into play before, during and after our actions.

The church fathers put it this way:

> In the depths of his conscience, man detects a law
> which he does not impose upon himself, but which
> holds him to obedience. Always summoning him
> to love good and to do it and to avoid evil, the voice
> of conscience can when necessary speak to his heart
> more specifically: do this, shun that. For man has
> in his heart a law written by God. To obey it is the
> very dignity of man: according to it he will be
> judged (*Pastoral Constitution on the Church in
> the Modern World,* 16).

Implicit in this description of the church fathers are the following
three points:

> 1. At one level, conscience refers to the struggle
> that goes on when we are faced with some particular
> decision as to what is right and what is wrong. It
> helps us sift through the data in trying to decide
> the human or right course of action. It is our own
> personal judgment, and we alone are responsible
> for doing the right thing and avoiding the wrong
> thing. (For example, in the drug case, conscience
> will enable Tom to make a decision as to what he
> should do with his friend Jack.)

> 2. At another level, conscience refers to a more
> general knowledge of right and wrong. It is the law
> which is written on our hearts, as referred to by
> the church fathers. It is the basic starting point that
> we all can discover about what is human, what is
> good. Ideas such as "be just," "honor the truth,"
> "respect life" are principles which are included in
> this law. (Again, in the drug case, Tom's con-
> science will enable him to ask himself the question
> "What is the human thing here?")

> 3. At still another level, conscience refers to a
> person's self-awareness as a child of God, how one
> ought to be in light of who he or she is. It can dis-
> cover our basic dignity as God's children and it
> commands us to be who we are. It helps us dis-
> cover that we should become more fully human,

both by doing good and avoiding evil. Christians believe that God is more present to us than we are to ourselves. He is within our hearts; he cares for us; he loves us. He invites us to accept his invitation of friendship and love, and calls us to act as his children in what we do. A person with a mature conscience will prayerfully listen to that call and act in accordance with it. (Finally, Tom's conscience can prompt him to do the loving thing in accordance with his basic dignity as a child of God.)

The common thread uniting these descriptions of conscience is that conscience is a kind of knowledge (science) which helps us know right from wrong and helps us decide in a particular situation to choose according to what is best for us as human beings, made in the image and likeness of God. If a person has a poorly formed conscience, he or she may choose the wrong thing without knowing it. The key to a well-formed conscience is to be open to new knowledge, new insights. The essence of a healthy conscience is that it is sensitive to all the elements of the STOP sign.

In conclusion, doing the right thing means following your conscience. To insure that you are doing the right thing, you should continuously be open, listening, consulting, praying. To go against what your conscience tells you to do is to sin. The topic of sin will be treated in Chapter 7.

Exercise:

Apply what you read in this section and the last one to the lifeboat case and to the drug case.

SUMMARY:

1. The Christian who is trying to do the right thing will seek help and guidance from the church, which is entrusted with the Lord's teaching authority.

2. Sifting out and assigning priorities to the conflicting values in a moral decision can often give insight into which value to choose in doing the right thing.

3. Trusting one's gut reaction to a particular situation might give strong illumination on what is the right thing to do.

4. In the last analysis, one must follow one's conscience. One must act. Understood, of course, is that one has developed and is developing one's conscience.

Some additional exercises:

1. Here is a good "conscience case." Imagine that you are a newspaper columnist who writes advice to troubled people. The following letter is mailed to you. Write a response to it. Because of space limitations, you may write no more than 150 words.

   Dear ——————————,
   You have got to help me. I need the advice of someone who doesn't know me. Last night, I was at the house of a friend. We have been friends since third grade. We went to her room. When there, my friend took out several valuable items she had shoplifted. She bragged about her exploits, claiming that she has stolen $500 worth of merchandise in the past three months. What worries me is that her parents are wealthy and she has plenty of money.

   Most of what she took she can't even use.

   She made me promise not to tell anyone. I know there is something wrong with her, but I don't know what to do. Maybe I should, for her own good. I'm really confused. Can you please help me?
   —Scared Sally

2. Put yourself into this situation:

   You come from a close-knit family. You love your parents very much and have never done anything to hurt them. They are very proud of you.

   However, as you approach graduation, it becomes clearer to you that you would like to become a teacher who works with handicapped children. You have been tutoring handicapped kids on a volunteer basis for two years and find much meaning in that kind of work. You want to go off to college to prepare for this kind of career.

But your father in particular has made it known that he wants you to study for a business degree so that you can take over his lucrative business. When you tell him of your college plans, he mentions that he is greatly disappointed in you and that if you intend to persist in your plans he will not help you with your expensive college education. You plead with him, but he will not bend.

What will you do? Explain your decision.

    a. What factors influenced your decision?

    b. Do parents have an obligation to educate their children through college? Explain.

5

The STOP Sign Applied

*So the Lord God cast a deep sleep on the man, and while
he was asleep, he took out one of his ribs and closed up
its place with flesh. The Lord God then built up into a
woman the rib that he had taken from the man. When he
brought her to the man, the man said:*

> *This one, at last, is bone of my bones and
> flesh of my flesh; This one shall be called
> "woman," for out of "her man" this one has
> been taken.*

*That is why a man leaves his father and mother and
clings to his wife, and the two of them become one body*
(Gn 2:21-24).

The moral decision-making process known as the STOP sign
has been treated in the past three chapters. The present chapter
will apply the method to a moral problem that young people ask
both themselves and others very often. The question takes many
forms. "What is the morality of premarital sex?" is a common
phrasing of the question. Equally common are "How far can I go
in the area of sex?" and "What, if anything, is considered wrong
in the area of sexual morality?" Let us take a look at these questions in light of the STOP sign. The whole process will require
that you get involved by asking some questions of yourself, by
filling in some exercises, by discussing with your classmates and
your teacher. By involving yourself in the chapter this way, perhaps the conclusions drawn will make more sense to you.

111

Before applying the STOP sign to the question of premarital sex, it is important to point out that all of us are in the process of growth, of movement forward, of integration. What this chapter will present is the *ideal* of Christian morality in the area of sexuality. We should never be discouraged because we sometimes fail to live that ideal. Rather, we should be aware of the wholeness we wish to achieve with the help of God. We are pilgrim people on our way to the Father. He knows that we are weak and subject to temptation. He calls us not to hate ourselves when we fall but to get up and try again. In addition, problems in the area of sex are often symptoms of other issues like insecurity, lack of love in family life and the like. It is important to realize these truths before looking at the ideal of sexual morality we are called to live as Christians.

SEARCH

The approach to any moral issue should always begin with a search for the facts. Let us apply the five "W's" and the "H" questions to the issue at hand.

What? The *what* concerns premarital sex; this is the moral object under consideration. But a further issue here concerns a definition of premarital sex. What are we talking about? Before passing judgment on the morality of premarital sex, we must know precisely what issue is being discussed. Are we talking about masturbation? Impure thoughts? Hand-holding? Kissing? Petting? "Going all the way"? In other words, what is the precise issue of premarital sex under consideration?

It is certainly understandable why these kinds of questions would be phrased in these ways. These kinds of questions are really asking "Where should we draw the line?" By separating the premarital sex issue into various components like those mentioned above, a person is really asking for guidelines. This is certainly good and understandable. However, there is usually another question that lurks behind these drawing-the-line kinds of questions and that is "How far can we go before we commit a mortal sin?"

The trouble with this question, however, is that the emphasis is too negative. It seeks to find loopholes and reflects a wrong emphasis in approaching the whole issue of sexual morality.

Is there a better way to get at the topic so that the discussion and study of it will be more positively treated? The following two questions can prove a bit more helpful in analyzing this topic, namely: What is appropriate behavior for me? What behavior truly represents my relationship and commitment? By emphasizing appropriateness of behavior, relationship and commitment the *what* of premarital sex is put into a larger picture. These are the kinds of questions we will approach in this chapter, and we will comment on some specific "where-do-we-draw-the-line?" questions along the way.

Why? Motive is an important question to answer in every area of morality. These are some of the possible motives involved when the why question is applied to premarital sex:

- for the release of tension
- because it feels good
- to use another person for one's own pleasure
- to dominate another person, that is, conquer him or her
- to share myself in love with another
- to build up my own self-image
- to overcome loneliness
- to experiment

Certainly, some of these reasons are good ones; others are clearly wrong. For example, sex with love as a primary motive seems to fit in well with the very nature of friendship and good relationships with others. But the essential issue is: Is premarital sex *loving?* What is the loving thing to do before marriage? Sex engaged in selfishly is like any other selfish act—wrong. With any human act, a person can have good motives, bad motives or mixed motives. A bad or selfish motive would make us suspect immediately that the action one proposes to do is wrong. Is this to say, however, that a good intention automatically makes an action right? There is a wise old saying that the road to hell is paved with good intentions. "I'm doing it to show love to another" is surely a good motive and in stark contrast to a motive of exploiting another. However, does such a worthy intention (which may well be mixed with selfish motives, too) make premarital sex right? Let us proceed.

Who? Involved in all moral issues is a "who," a person. In the case of premarital sex, the people involved could be close friends or strangers who hardly know each other. In the latter case, one can easily see how the relationship would be casual and most probably engaged in just to use the other, to treat the other as object. To treat any person as an object is not to treat the person with dignity and respect. Thus, it is clear that casual, promiscuous sex is wrong; it dehumanizes. People are turned into anonymous things; they lose their individuality. At least an argument could be made that a sexual relationship with a friend out of love is less wrong than an exploitative one with a stranger. We are narrowing our topic a bit, but we have only begun to approach it.

When and Where? The timing is important here because we are asking the question is sex *before* marriage moral? The assumption is that a healthy, loving sexual relationship between a husband and wife is good. We are concerned about the question of the rightness of sexual relations before marriage. At first glance, the *where* does not look that significant here since the question is really focused on another reality. Where is important, though, because it can contribute to occasions of engaging in premarital sex. A couple who finds themselves in places and at a time (the when) which make it very easy to engage in a sexual relationship are really adding to the potential moral problem. If indeed premarital sex is immoral, then a person ought to avoid places and times that can add to the temptation.

How? A person could easily mean two things by this question: What techniques are involved and what degree of caring do you bring to the action? It is not necessary here to comment on the first question other than to say mankind's imagination has probably exhausted most of the possibilities. Certain of these are clearly unbefitting humans. For example, bestiality (relations with an animal) is one example. Rape is still another example. As to the second question, one could easily dismiss as immoral sexual activity, those actions engaged in which are uncaring, harmful or exploitative of another person.

Summary of the Search. Without yet delving into a deep analysis of the nature of premarital sex, asking the 5 W's and the H can at least indicate that some sexual activity is wrong. For example:

1. Using sex selfishly by dominating or exploiting another is wrong. These are bad motives. However, even good intentions do not make sex (or any other action) right.

2. Engaging in sex casually, and thus treating a person as an object, is wrong. Persons are individuals worthy of respect and dignity. Sex can be used to exploit strangers. (It can also be used to exploit friends, as we shall see.)

3. If premarital sex is wrong, then places and times that may occasion it should be avoided.

4. Certain sexual acts are unbefitting humans. Among these would be bestiality and rape.

Liberal vs. conservative views of sex.

Below are statements about sex which have been held or are held by people in our society. Mark with a C or an L those statements that you think are too conservative or too liberal. Leave unmarked those statements which you believe give a correct description of human sexuality.

—— Sex is only for fun.

—— Sex is only for procreation.

—— Sex is sinful.

—— Only men enjoy sex; women tolerate it.

—— "Living together" is OK.

—— Kissing is wrong except for married couples.

—— Virginity is an old-fashioned word.

—— Abortion on demand is OK.

—— Having kids is too much trouble.

—— Having kids is the only reason to get married.

—— Women are asking for trouble when they wear immodest clothes.

—— Nudity makes you free.

—— People should be allowed to wear whatever they want.

Discuss your responses with your classmates and teacher.

THINK

The next part of the STOP sign prompts us to ask about the alternatives and the consequences.

A consideration of alternatives and consequences takes a considerable amount of thought. Reason, however, is often clouded if not blinded when premarital sex takes place. Hence, it is very difficult if not impossible at times to look at questions in this area rationally when a person is emotionally involved. For example, have you ever tried to talk an "involved" couple out of a marriage which was doomed in the eyes of all except the couple? Emotions rule without reason. Thus, it is all the more important to think about the issues before getting involved emotionally.

What are the alternatives? Unfortunately, there is a very strong attitude in contemporary American society which fosters the notion that you are strange, weird, ultraconservative and stupid if you do not engage in sexual intercourse whenever and with whomever you want. This attitude is fostered on television shows which portray 16-year-olds "maturing" by having a sexual adventure, in movies which almost always have sex or violence as one of their themes, in explicit song lyrics that "tell it like it is," and on mindless talk shows that do not even consider that the prevailing customs just might be wrong. One stark example was a recent television talk show which supposedly had a debate on the morality of today. A professor from Fordham University was trying to share church teaching on sex and other moral issues. When he mentioned words like "self-control" and "chastity," the audience actually laughed at him. Laughed at him! The implication was that he was so "out of it" that he was humorous.

The truth of it is, however, that to be really human is to see more than one way to approach reality, even if the crowd of people sees it just the one way. In the area of premarital sex, a viable option is to respect the other person (as well as self) and save the intimacy of sexual relationship for marriage. To say that humans cannot control their desires and urges is to say that they are like animals which are determined by the laws of nature. In the Christian tradition, we give people more credit than that. We believe that a young couple can relate as friends, grow in a relationship and be affectionate without sharing the total intimacy which should be reserved only for marriage. This is a viable alternative. A chaste life before marriage, that is, one which respects one's own and another's sexuality and does not abuse it, is the ideal possibility and norm of Christian morality. It is the real alternative Christians try to live. It is an option that should be considered and acted on.

What are the consequences? What are the effects of pre-marital sex? Here are some of them, under the categories of physical, emotional and spiritual effects.

Physical effects. Obviously, sexual activity feels good. It is one of the greatest physical pleasures God gave to us. Secondly, it can make us feel close to a person. A third feeling which can result is a feeling of frustration. This happens when sexual excitation begins and is not completed. It also happens when a person realizes that what took place is not in the context of a permanent relationship and is thus passing. Outside of marriage, sex can also bring about the physical consequences of unwanted pregnancies or social diseases.

Emotional effects. In a premarital context, sexual activity like intercourse can bring about the impression that one has been used. This happens especially when a person declares his or her "love," only to end the relationship when somebody else comes along. Sharing and communicating sexually is sharing and communicating on a very deep level. Emotions are deeply involved. As a result, a person can be easily hurt, so hurt, in fact, that one might be very reluctant to open to another person again for fear of more hurt. A long-term emotional effect which can be carried even into marriage is a distrust of the sincerity of another. If a person has been hurt, the question in the back of his or her mind might well be, "Does the other really care about me as a person?" Finally, guilt feelings are often tied up with sex used outside marriage.

Spiritual consequences. As we shall see later, sexual activity is a share in God's own creative life. It touches at the very heart of what it means to be a human and how we relate to others and God. By improperly using sex (within or outside of marriage) one can easily alienate himself or herself from God. Improper use of our sexuality can close us off from true love; it can make us selfish, self-centered. It can keep us from growing. On the other hand, proper use of sex enables us to grow close to the one we love, close to all people with whom we have contact and close to our Lord.

Summary of "Think." A serious consideration of alternatives to premarital sex would hold that people can find creative ways of relating to others without, for example, "going all the way." A healthy integrative approach to sex is an alternative that should at least be considered. Like all human actions, proper use of sex has its good effects, improper use of sex its bad effects. These should be considered when judging the morality of premarital sex.

Sex Inventory:

1. As a class, list at least 3 other consequences of improper use of sex. Discuss these.

   a.

   b.

   c.

2. How do you feel when somebody talks about sex as though it were only an activity?

3. Bring to class at least three ads which exploit the theme of sex. Share and discuss these.

4. Do you agree that contemporary song lyrics are too explicit about sex? Explain.

5. Check which of the following *feelings* you think sex can express:

   —— hatred

   —— bitterness

   —— inner peace

   —— joy

   —— guilt

   —— love

   —— anger

   —— loneliness

   —— routineness (the "blahs")

   Explain your choices. Which of the above emotions *ought* sex to express in a healthy relationship?

OTHERS

Sexual morality, like the morality of all our actions, involves other people. In addition, the advice of others can be very helpful in trying to decide the right thing to do.

Consider others. By our very nature, we are sexual beings. Male and female God created us; in his image he created us. The term "sexual relations" implies rather strongly the concept of other people. Others are always involved where sex comes into play. This is true for both thoughts and deeds. Our thoughts, for example, can direct us to see others as objects to be possessed or as persons to be loved. Even our private sexual acts have social dimensions. An act of self-centered love, masturbation, for example, has a tendency to close us in on ourselves. It makes us less open in relating to others.

As we saw in our discussion of the emotional effects of sexual activity, sex can be a powerful way of expressing love—or of using another person. Surely, the feelings and well-being of others ought to be considered before engaging in sex of any kind. Might what I propose to do be harmful to others? Might it hurt them? Might it merely use them? Might it turn the other into an object for my pleasure and not someone who is to be respected and cherished for what he or she is? These are some of the questions that must be asked if one is sincere about a true examination of one's motives.

Consult others. An earlier chapter discussed the value of principles discovered by others who have gone before us and which are shared with those who come after them. We owe it to our parents, teachers, and other adults to discover their reasons for the sexual morality they teach. The philosopher George Santayana said that those who refuse to learn from history are condemned to repeat the mistakes of the past. In the area of sexual morality, it is possible that a person who ignores the guidelines and wisdom which those more experienced have learned (maybe from their own mistakes) are perhaps doomed to repeat the very same mistakes.

A good guideline in forming one's sexual morality is at least to talk over one's ideas with a trusted adult, one who feels comfortable with his or her own sexuality. The insights, the understanding and the support such a person can give might prove invaluable.

Others and Sex:

With whom do you feel comfortable talking over questions dealing with sex?

—— a parent

—— a favorite teacher

—— a counselor

—— a priest or confessor

—— a close friend of either sex

—— a relative

—— some other adult

My attitude toward the older generation's view of sex is:

—— It is hypocritical—they don't practice what they preach.

—— It is old-fashioned and not meaningful for today.

—— It has value and is worth listening to.

—— I don't know enough about it to pass judgment.

Discuss your reaction to the second checklist.

PRAY

The beauty of prayer is that it puts us in contact with our Lord, a Lord who was a man like us in everything but sin. Here was a real man, a flesh-and-bones man, a man who knew what it was like to be tempted, a man who knew what it was like to know desire, a man who knew how to love. Jesus was the one who understood failure—wasn't he the one who forgave the adulteress who was so quick to be condemned by her accusers? Wasn't he the one who could look on his apostle Peter with forgiving eyes after Peter had denied knowing him? Wasn't he the one who dined with sinners?

Jesus understands us, our problems, our joys and strong desires better than anyone. He knows how his Father made us. He knows the kind of society we live in. He knows what he has asked of us.

Jesus is the one who promised that he would be with us, ready to help us. Jesus is the one who promised to send his Spirit to guide us and strengthen us. Jesus is the one who stands ready to enter our hearts if we but turn to him and receive him.

Our Lord stands ready to help us, guide and strengthen us, in all difficult decisions, and to forgive us if need be; we need but turn to him. Our greatest resource in working out a sexual morality is the man-God who knows us, our weaknesses and strengths better than we do ourselves. There is only one catch, though: we must be willing to ask for his help—freely and often.

For reflection:

When was the last time you prayed?

Have you ever asked our Lord's help in understanding your sexuality?

For discussion:

How many people in our country today do you think believe what you just read in this last section? Why or why not?

JESUS

A careful reading of the New Testament can give some interesting insights on our topic. Concerning sexual morality, Jesus seemed to extol the virtues of marital love. He compared God's kingdom with a wedding banquet. His first miracle was at the wedding feast at Cana. Jesus himself was compared to a bridegroom; his church is the bride. In connection with this, he elevated the position of women in the society of his day. Women were often treated as second-class citizens, unequal to men under the Jewish law. For example, up to his day, men had great ease in "putting away" (that is, divorcing) their wives. Jesus forbade divorce. In other words, Jesus treated women with respect and dignity and reaffirmed the sacredness of marital love. His love for women as persons (not objects) was illustrated by the mercy he showed to the woman caught in adultery and to the woman who anointed him at the house of the Pharisee. He numbered them among his closest friends; for example, after his resurrection he appeared first to Mary Magdalene. He associated with them publicly when this was frowned upon; for example, when he met the Samaritan woman at the well. He used them in his parables. In one of them, he compared a woman who found a coin to God the Father who rejoices when a sinner repents. Jesus went out of his way to show men that women deserve love and respect.

As we saw in an earlier chapter, Jesus put a lot of emphasis on motives in morality. He said that what makes a person impure is not so much the action but what comes from the heart (Mt 15:1-20). A careful examination of one's motives in the area of sex helps keep one from self-deception. We must remember, too, the two questions: Is this a loving action? Is this a serving action? Love here means treating the other as one would like to be treated. Is this act I propose to do a loving one? Does it help the other or is it self-serving? Am I merely doing it for my own pleasure or to build up my own ego? The honest answer to these questions can go a long way in helping a person decide the right thing to do in the area of sexual morality.

The Ideal Man/Woman

In speaking about marriage as an ideal, it is good sometimes to reflect on who an ideal marriage partner might
be. Reflect on the following: My ideal of the perfect
male/female is one who—

stands for:

reminds me of:

is good at:

has eyes like:

would like to:

refuses to:

looks like:

admires:

has fun at:

cares for me by:

REASON AND REVELATION

Reason and revelation shed much light on the morality of sexual actions.

Reason. Human reason attempts to discover an answer to the question, "What is the *human* thing to do?" The implication here is that in the area of sex there is a human thing to do. Human sexual acts are not merely animal behavior. They are not primarily animal stimulus-response acts of tension release. If they were, there would be no need to discuss their morality. Human acts tell us about humans; they reveal something about what it means to be a body-person with a mind and free will and in relationship to others.

The traditional way of approaching the morality of sexual acts is to look at their purpose. What is sexual activity for? Generally, two purposes of sexual activity can be noted: it is *life-giving* and *love-communicating*. Our creator made us separate ("sex" is derived from a word which means "to split"), complementary persons. He has given us a share in procreating life. That marvelous share is our sexual faculty. Ultimately, it is designed to bring children into existence. It is a great gift. But for humans it is also a profound way to share love, to show concern, to communicate at the most intimate level. These two purposes go hand in hand: in the ideal order, children are the manifestation of love between the parents.

According to this reasoning, using our sexual faculty correctly implies that it be within the context of giving life and giving love. To use it incorrectly is to exclude one of its purposes. Furthermore, the instability of sexual love seems to speak very strongly for some institution that will help keep two lovers faithful to each other. Marriage is such an institution. In a marriage, a couple promises to themselves and to the human community that they will remain faithful (unto death) in their sharing of life and love. Marriage, in other words, helps stabilize a relationship of life and love shared between a couple.

Using the sexual faculty outside of marriage is to distort its meaning. Sexual intercourse, for example, is a powerful symbol of the *total* giving and receiving between the husband and wife. Unless there is a total giving and receiving, one cannot have intercourse. As a human act, it communicates a total loving between the two. In a marriage, the partners have promised to give themselves to each other exclusively and permanently. In a marriage, the act of intercourse reinforces that love which brings forth life. It is a symbol which truly communicates what it is supposed to communicate.

Outside of a marriage, the use of the sexual faculty is a misuse because it does not symbolize, that is, communicate total love in a context of giving life. A couple engaging in premarital sex has not really committed themselves totally to each other. They have not promised to be faithful and true. There is always a string attached that one can get out of the relationship if inconvenience comes along. Thus, sexual intercourse before marriage is a seriously wrong use of a profound human symbol for love. It is a "strings attached" kind of relationship which in reality is not truthful. It manifests more than what is present in the relationship. It is incomplete and distorts the meaning of giving and receiving love unconditionally. So, too, acts which lead up to intercourse are frustrating and not representative of true, total love. Petting to orgasm, for example, might be very pleasurable, but it is ultimately frustrating; it blocks true love in a context of giving life. It does not communicate the care, respect and fidelity which ought to be in the act. Masturbation, too, is a lonely act of self-love, closed to the giving of life and the sharing of love. These acts are seriously wrong because they distort the profound meaning of the sexual nature given to us by the Creator. (Whether they are sinful or not, as we shall see in Chapter 7, depends on one's knowledge and freedom.)

Thus, a moral use of sex according to our reason is one that will be reserved for the kind of commitment which is total and open to life. That kind of commitment is present only in marriage where the relationship is one of total giving and receiving with *no* strings attached.

Revelation. The Old Testament sees sex as basically good. God created humans male and female in his image and saw that what he had created was very good. This chapter opened with the quote from Genesis about the creation of woman. In this story, we see that from the beginning the notion of mutuality, of sharing in love, is a central theme in mankind's sexual nature. Eve was created to fulfill Adam, to make him complete, to overcome his loneliness. Humanity is incomplete without the feminine dimension. Man and woman were made to complement each other. The Old Testament authors often refer to marital love as a symbol for the covenant love between Yahweh and the Jewish people. When Israel was unfaithful to the special love Yahweh showered on her, she was compared to an adulteress. The lovely Song of Songs is a marvelous piece of literature that highly sings the praises of sexual love within the context of marriage. Unlike many of the cultures which surrounded the nation of Israel, the Jews saw sex as a great good created by God, to be enjoyed within the context of marriage. What the Jews were quick to condemn were certain sexual abuses practiced by their pagan neighbors, abuses like prostitution which did not befit the dignity of a human person.

In the New Testament, the great St. Paul also found it necessary to condemn certain sexual abuses. He wrote to recent converts to Christianity, many of whom had a hard time giving up their former pagan sexual practices. For Paul, the Christian had a special dignity as a member incorporated into the Body of Christ. Thus, certain sexual practices were seen by St. Paul as being unbecoming a Christian who was a temple of the Holy Spirit. In his first letter to the Corinthians, Paul directly condemns fornication (premarital sexual intercourse), prostitution, adultery, homosexuality and lewd conduct. These actions are incompatible with the Christian vocation of mirroring Christ in the world.

One final comment is in order here. As we have seen, the human person is a unity composed of both matter (body) and spirit. Human sexual expression ought to express this unity of person. Selfish sexual expression tends to separate the spiritual aspects of a person from his or her body. In selfish sex, the person is treated as an object and not as an individual who reflects God's love. Any time a person is not treated as a unity, both body and soul, exploitation takes place. This failure to relate to another as a full person, worthy of respect and love, is wrong because of the depersonalization that takes place. St. Paul writes of this reality in 1 Cor:

> Shun lewd conduct. Every other sin a man commits is outside his body, but the fornicator sins against his own body. You must know that your body is a temple of the Holy Spirit, who is within—the Spirit you have received from God. You are not your own. You have been purchased, and at a price. So glorify God in your body (I Cor 6:18-20).

Conclusion. Human reason can discover that the nature of sexual love is both life-giving and love-sharing. Within the context of marriage, both purposes of sexual activity can be achieved; outside of marriage, one or the other purpose is frustrated so that the sexual relationship does not indicate a true commitment of love and life-sharing. Thus, premarital sex is a distortion of what should be a powerful symbol of human love. Both the Old and New Testaments condemn certain sexual activity as unbecoming the dignity of the human person. St. Paul explicitly condemns fornication, that is, premarital sexual intercourse, as unbecoming a member of Christ's body and a temple of the Holy Spirit.

The Meaning of Love

When you think of love, what primarily comes to mind?

—— a feeling

—— an attraction

—— a giving

—— an instinct

—— a commitment

—— friendship

What does it mean to love unconditionally? What are some of the limiting conditions which of necessity are present in a relationship outside of marriage?

In what way is sexual love communication? Explain?

IMAGINATION

Because so many elements of our society leave very little room for imagination when it comes to sexual love, you might conclude that imagination has little to bear on this topic. In reality, though, it does. Where creative imagination is most needed is for non-married friends to discover ways to enrich their friendship without "going all the way." Developing a solid friendship upon which a more intimate relationship can later be based is not easy and takes much effort and work. But if a marriage is to work, the husband and wife must be best of friends. It is the nature of erotic (sexual) love to be blinded by passion; it refuses to see the other as he or she really is. Friendship, on the other hand, recognizes the truth about the other. By sharing common interests, by getting to know one another, by developing many friendships, young people can prepare for a stable relationship in marriage. This takes a lot of work and a lot of imagination especially in a culture which actively fosters sex as the solution to all problems and the magic key to happiness. This, of course, is the great lie sold to us. If it were the key, then we would have many more happy marriages and a lot less divorce. Happiness results from fidelity, self-control and total sharing. Unless these virtues are built up before the total self-commitment of marriage, it will be very difficult to discover them later.

For discussion:

1. Why do you think the divorce rate is so high?

2. How do advertisements foster the notion of self-indulgence? Find some ads which push this theme.

3. If you were a parent giving advice to a young person about responsible growth in friendship with a member of the opposite sex, what would you say?

LAW

Many of the principles governing sexual morality which would normally be treated under this heading have already been discussed. For example, "natural law" arguments governing the topic of pre-marital sex are the same as those discussed under the topic of reason. Likewise, under the category of Jesus and revelation, divine law was basically covered. What needs to be mentioned here are the values taught in the sixth and ninth Commandments. These Commandments seek to praise the virtue of chastity both in action and attitude. Modesty is an important help in fostering a healthy attitude to sex. It goes without saying that certain forms of dress, dancing, conversation, entertainment and the like, can strongly influence one's attitude and behavior in sexual matters. Christian modesty helps a person govern his or her behavior in a way that is responsive to one's vocation as a child of God. Certainly, styles change and what was offensive in the past or in another place may not be today. This is not to say, however, that all behavior is acceptable. At times, the Christian must stand against the culture in which he or she lives and proclaim the sacredness and true beauty of the human person and argue against false attempts to debase and cheapen the person.

Civil law probably does not enter the picture for this topic except in the case of statutory rape. Statutory rape is a criminal offense in most states when an older person engages in sexual relations with a minor, despite the consent of the minor.

Church law will not be discussed here. Much of what the church has to say about sex is spoken of in the context of marriage and marital love and not under the category of law as such. We will discuss the creative insights of the church in the next section of the chapter.

Discuss:

1. Are laws designed by society to protect the young from seduction a good idea? Why or why not?

2. Should there be laws to govern what a person wears in public? governing pornography? why or why not?

CHURCH

In forming his or her conscience, the Catholic will pay special attention to the teaching of the church. Because human sexuality is such an important issue for human beings, and deals with their relationship to others in the transmission of life, it is a topic of concern on which the church has often taught. Here are some of the principles behind the church's teaching:

1. The church has continuously taught (and, at times, against considerable opposition) that human sexuality is a basic human good. Human sexuality is not merely genital activity, but also an aspect of our personality which lets us enter into the lives of others as friends and encourages them to enter our lives. Concerning sexual intercourse as the full expression of human love, in his encyclical *Humanae Vitae,* Pope Paul VI admirably summed up church teaching in one sentence:

> Husband and wife, through that mutual gift of themselves which is properly theirs and exclusive to them alone, develop that union of two persons in which they perfect one another, in order to cooperate with God in the generation and education of new lives (n. 8).

2. The Vatican's *Declaration on Certain Questions Concerning Sexual Ethics* (1975) teaches that genuine moral behavior flows from one's internal conviction, and is not primarily imposed by external authority. *Genuine moral response* flows from within a person's heart and is not forced by external power. Applied to sexual ethics, a person must freely choose the value of conforming his or her life to Christ Jesus who is the ultimate, objective norm for judging human sexuality. In its life-giving and love-sharing capabilities, in its joy and playfulness, in its positive contribution to human growth, a person must ask how the various ways of sexual expression can help foster growth in Christ. Respect and love, combined with a study of the nature of human actions involved, help us discover God's will for us in human sexual expression.

3. In her vocation as Christ's presence in the world, the

church has consistently taught the specific guidelines for sexual morality as discussed under the sections above, especially Jesus, reason and revelation. To reiterate here, the church has been faithful to scripture by insisting that love of God is incompatible with every form of fornication, sexual promiscuity and uncleanness, sensuality and licentiousness, lustful desires, incest, homosexual actions and other sexual perversions.

4. Finally, the church, composed of members of Christ's body, lives in the world. She knows that she proposes an ideal. She knows how difficult it is to live the ideal in a sex-saturated and a sinful world where mistakes will be made and sins will be committed in the name of love. As a result, the church lends her support, her love and prayers, her care and the forgiveness of Christ to young people (and to all others) in their difficult struggle of trying to integrate a healthy sexual morality into their lives. The church offers a challenge to all Christians to live a life which is different. The church recognizes that to be different, that is, to be a follower of Christ in the area of sexual morality, is a challenge which meets many obstacles. The promise, however, is one of fidelity to the word of God and to one's call as God's special people who witness to the love of a God who cares for all people.

A Group Exercise:

1. With your classmates, compose a list giving the pros and cons of premarital sexual intercourse. As a class, narrow the list to the two most representative reasons for abstaining from sexual intercourse before marriage and the two most representative reasons for indulging.

Each person, then, should ask both his or her parents and one other married couple to comment on the list. Share their reflections in a class discussion.

2. Imagine that you have a 13-year-old brother and that you discover that he occasionally is having sexual intercourse with a girl his age. What would you do? What advice would you give him? What if the person involved was not a brother but a sister? If you gave advice, would it equally apply to a person your age? Why or why not?

VALUES and INSTINCT

There are a number of values that can be identified in this issue of premarital sex. The exercise you have just completed may have helped you uncover some of these values. On the side of not engaging in premarital sexual activity are values like chastity, fidelity to the word of God, respect for one's own sexuality and that of another, self-control, friendship and agape love. On the other side of the spectrum, the value of immediate pleasure and the closeness one can achieve physically with another are most prominent. These values should be considered and ranked. Furthermore, it should be pointed out that a number of false values have already been noted when one engages in premarital sex. Among these false values would be the possible use of another, unfaithfulness to God's word, self-indulgence, "going along with the crowd," and the many potential harmful effects discussed above.

On first glance, one's gut reaction or instinct might very well be to engage in the pleasure of the moment. Our feelings will often direct us to seek pleasure in the "now." These feelings are normal, natural and good. That does not mean, though, that they should necessarily be paid attention to. At the same time, however, most everyone who is contemplating premarital sexual relations senses that he or she might be doing something wrong. This second gut-level reaction cannot be denied. Proof of it is the great concern people have in trying to justify their behavior and the guilt feelings they might have. Merely asking the question, "How far can I go?" reflects a deep-felt intuition that there just might be something that is not right about intimate sexual relations before the commitment of marriage. This sense of uneasiness may prompt a person to consider that sex is sacred because it is a share in the creation of life and in a total giving in friendship. As in the case of values, these feelings should be felt, weighed and judged in light of the other data revealed by the STOP sign.

To consider:

Do you agree with the observations just made? Why or why not? Can you add to them?

Here is another values exercise. Again, imagine that someone is writing to you for advice. What would you say?

Dear ———————————,

How do you know when you are going too far with a boy? Boys are very different. If you say or act one way with one boy he reacts one way. If you say or do the same thing with another he gets all kinds of ideas. I am a virgin and would like to stay that way. I do like to show affection and be nice to the guys I date, but only so far. What is the best way to understand male psychology and where should I draw the line?

—Worried Wendy

This letter is from a parent.

Dear ———————————,

My 15-year-old asked me about birth control devices yesterday. I did not know she was even interested in this topic. I'm worried that if I tell her too much she might take advantage of the knowledge. What should I do?

—A concerned parent

CONSCIENCE

A person's conscience will enable him or her to decide on the issue of premarital sex. Recall the two principles of conscience: a person must both develop it and follow it. Taking the trouble and effort to find out about a moral issue like premarital sex and always being open to new data is a very good indication that a person is sincere about informing his or her conscience. Likewise, deciding for oneself (that is, not following the crowd) and doing what one's conscience dictates as the right thing *is* the true test of following one's conscience. In the last analysis, a person is responsible for his or her actions. By doing what his or her conscience dictates in this area, as well as in all other areas of life, a person assumes responsibility.

In concluding this chapter, you may wish to consider a few more points that are relevant to this topic of premarital sex. They might be helpful in forming your judgment about the topic:

1. Sex is a great good given to us by our Creator. In the midst of all the false values sold to us today, we should never forget that sex is not the cheap, commercial thing that so many people wish to make it. Furthermore, the sexual feelings that we possess should never be looked at as bad or to be feared. God made us as we are and blessed us with the feelings we have. They are natural. We should recognize their source and be thankful that we have been given a share in bringing new life into the world.

2. Showing affection to a friend is good. Embraces, kissing, touching are all important signs of sharing friendship and expressing love for another person. We need but remember two things: 1) Sexual feelings are powerful and yearn for fulfillment. It is difficult to reverse strong sexual feeling once excited. 2) Thus, we should be careful and respectful of both our own feelings and those of another. What does not affect one person may be a serious temptation to another. What is demanded here is caution and respect for self and others.

3. Failures in the area of sexual morality ought never give rise to feelings of self-hatred. Our Lord stands ready to accept us. He knows how difficult it is to live a chaste life. On the other hand, he requires it of his followers and will give his strength and help to those who are ready to receive it.

SUMMARY

1. An examination of the five W's (What, Why, Who, Where, When) and the H (How) reveals that some kinds of sexual activity are clearly unbecoming for humans: actions like bestiality, rape, promiscuous sex, exploitation of another, etc.

2. Despite contemporary notions to the contrary, engaging in premarital sex is not the only alternative open to young people. Like all human actions, sexual activity has its consequences: physical, emotional and spiritual.

3. Responsible sex always is considerate of the feelings of others. Others, especially those more experienced and comfortable with their sexuality, can be helpful guides in forming one's conscience in the area of sexual morality.

4. Christians believe that prayer and the insights of Jesus are powerful helps in working out a sexual morality. Jesus would have us ask two questions: Is this a loving act? Is this a serving act?

5. Reason can discover that human sexual activity has the purpose of sharing love and giving life. Thus, to exclude either purpose would be to misuse sex. Outside marriage, one or the other purpose is almost always excluded. As a result, reason seems to indicate that premarital sex is wrong. Revelation praises the beauty and goodness of sex. Authors like St. Paul indicate that certain sexual activities (like fornication) are unbecoming for the Christian, a member of Christ's body.

6. Creative imagination helps in the developing of friendships which are based on more than just sexual attraction. It can aid in searching out ways to relate to another beyond the obvious ways suggested by contemporary culture.

7. For the Catholic, church teaching is a valuable guide in forming one's conscience in sexual matters. The church, trying to preserve the goodness of sex, has spoken often on the topic.

8. Ultimately, one is responsible for one's actions. A person must follow his or her conscience. This implies that he or she has formed it and is continually open to new insights. A person will be attentive to law, values and feelings. Furthermore, a Christian knows that to follow Jesus Christ often means to be different and to act in the right way, even if it is unpopular.

6

Moral Pluralism

The unexamined life is not worth living.
——Socrates

We live in a society where there is no one way to approach moral issues. Because there are *many* ways to approach moral problems, we call our society a *pluralistic* one, perhaps more so than any other in mankind's history. This fact alone has contributed to the crisis in morality that many people are feeling today. What is the right thing to do when no one can agree on what *the* right thing is? No issue points this out more dramatically than the controversial topic of abortion. Hardly a day goes by without a newspaper discussing this heated issue in one form or another.

What causes this confusion? More than anything else, there is widespread uncertainty over an issue like abortion because people have different ways of looking at reality. They disagree on what is the *human* thing to do. In fact, they even disagree on what it means to be human. They put an emphasis on one factor versus another factor and consequently come up with different conclusions.

This chapter will try to illustrate this problem of pluralism in ethics by discussing the topic of abortion. We will begin by looking at an imaginary debate on abortion among four different kinds of people. We will listen to their arguments and then discuss their starting points. Finally, the chapter will conclude with a few remarks about the Catholic position on this extremely important moral issue of today.

ABORTION—A Debate

Cast of Characters

> **Prof. Jones**—a doctor of philosophy at the local state university.
>
> **Ms. Smith**—a leader in the women's rights movement; an advocate of the Equal Rights Amendment.
>
> **Mr. Johnson**—a Catholic leader of the pro-life movement.
>
> **Sarah Williams**—a well-known journalist; known for her exposes of crime in high places; an atheist.

JONES: I'm for abortion in the following two cases: First, if abortion will help the mother for either physical or psychological reasons. Second, if abortion will be good for all the other people involved. For example, if abortion helps the problem of overpopulation, then it is OK.

SMITH: Like you, Prof. Jones, I see nothing wrong with abortion. A woman has the right to her own body. The fetus is part of the woman's body—a mass of cell tissue—she can have it taken out of her if she wants to. I don't see why people get all disturbed about abortion. They don't say anything about an operation on an appendix, why should they complain about abortion?

JOHNSON: I respect your opinions, Prof. Jones and Ms. Smith, but I think you are both wrong. Abortion, in my view and the view of my church, is a flagrant attack on innocent life. I can't think of any good reason why an innocent child's life should be taken.

SMITH: Where we differ, Mr. Johnson, is that you think a fetus is human life; I don't. You think it is murder to abort, I compare it to a reasonable medical operation.

JONES: You know, Mr. Johnson, Ms. Smith is right. To me it does not much matter if we are talking about human life or not. You cannot really prove if it is human life or not; I can't prove if it is merely cell tissue. The question of human life is a moot issue. What is important is what good the operation will do for either the individual or society. If the operation does good, it is OK; if the operation results in no good then I would not approve of it.

WILLIAMS: I agree with Prof. Jones and Ms. Smith on permitting abortion. We live in a dog-eat-dog world. My work has clearly shown me that those who survive are the fittest. If a woman wants to expel a parasite from her uterus, then she has every right to do so. It's the law of the land.

JOHNSON: Looks like mine is a minority position. I'll grant you that if a fetus is not human, then abortion would be as moral or immoral as any other operation under similar conditions. But I maintain that at the moment of conception we are dealing with human life. For example, when the female egg is fertilized, the entire genetic package of the person is determined. That rapidly developing cell cannot grow into anything but a human. We have a duty as fellow humans to care for that innocent life.

WILLIAMS: Wait a minute, Mr. Johnson. Who says we have a duty to help anyone other than ourselves? I just don't buy that. I'm responsible for myself and for myself alone.

JONES: Well, Sarah, I can't agree with you on that point. I do think the sign of a civilized nation is that it does protect the rights of others. It's just that I think that in certain situations the rights of the living mother and the good of society as a whole outweigh the rights (if we can say a fetus has rights) of the unborn. It's like the issue of self-defense. You Catholics have made a marvelous justification for allowing a person to kill another in self-defense. In that case, you say the rights of the unjust attacker are less than the person attacked. I think we have the same kind of case here.

JOHNSON: I simply cannot agree. Sure, there is a right to self-defense. But how can you call a fetus an unjust attacker?

SMITH: That's easy. The cell tissue is draining the mother of her strength and nutrients. If she does not want to be pregnant, then the mass of fetal tissue is "attacking her" and should be removed.

JOHNSON: Once again, Ms. Smith, you keep saying "a mass of cell tissue." You imply that a fetus is just a growth. I don't know how you can say that when, for example, between the 21st and 25th days, the tiny child already has eyes, a spinal cord, a nervous system, thyroid glands, lungs, stomach, liver, kidneys and intestines already developing. A head and brain are already developing. No, this is human life and not what you euphemistically call "cell tissue." The sign of a civilized nation is that it protects innocent life. And that, Prof. Jones, is what we are talking about: *innocent* life. There is a world of difference between the unjust assailant and a developing human child who is completely defenseless.

WILLIAMS: Oh, cut the sentimentality. Besides, abortion is legal in the United States. I get rather sick and tired of you Catholics and other pro-lifers forcing your morality down our throats.

SMITH: That's right, Johnson. No one is forcing a woman to get an abortion. A woman can freely choose. All I'm fighting for is to give the woman the right.

JOHNSON: I don't think I'm a bigot or a busybody in my fight to protect what I think is innocent life. In our country, the sign of a good citizen is to work for laws that will protect the innocent. The Supreme Court decision of 1973 is misguided and immoral even if it is legal. There is a higher law than human law and we are answerable to it.

WILLIAMS: I was waiting for him to bring in God. Well, I don't believe in God and I don't buy your argument. You Catholics are just trying to force your morality on others.

SMITH: I bet he'd change his tune if he was involved in an unwanted pregnancy. It is easy for a man to be against an abortion. We're talking about birth control and nothing else.

JONES: Yes, a dead fetus is better than an unwanted child.

JOHNSON: All I'm asking for is to give the child a chance to answer whether he or she wants to live. People talk about saving the child from the grief of living a life of not being wanted. I often wonder—without judging anyone—if that argument is just not an excuse to save the people involved from embarrassment, the cost of raising the child, or whatever. I'm not always sure there is a real concern for the child.

JONES: Well, we have expressed our views. I don't think we'll be getting anywhere if we debate this one further.

Exercise:

If you were Johnson, what else would you or should you have said?

Fact vs. Opinion

As in any moral issue, opinions which cannot be clearly proven are often mixed in with facts. This is the case with abortion. See if you can separate fact from opinion. Below are listed a number of positions and statements about abortion. Some are fact; some are opinion. Check (√) those statements which you think are facts. Put a + sign next to those which you think represent a good opinion. Put a − sign next to those which you think represent a bad opinion.

—— Abortion is wrong because it violates the fifth Commandment.

—— The fetus is not human.

—— The fetus is human.

—— Abortion is a form of genocide and thus immoral.

—— At the moment of conception, the fertilized egg has the total genetic program of a human being.

—— A dead fetus is better than an unwanted child.

—— If we allow abortion, then infanticide and euthanasia are just around the corner.

—— Abortion is a form of contraception.

—— A person is an authentic person when he or she can exercise individual freedom and can interact with others.

—— Because abortion is legal it is moral.

Discussion:

Can you come up with any logical arguments to "disprove" any of the opinion statements above?

An Analysis of the Debate

The following brief paragraphs will try to get at the under-lying assumptions held by the characters in our abortion debate. These represent different philosophies held by people in contemporary society.

1. *Prof. Jones.* Jones is a utilitarian. The philosophy of utilitarianism holds that the consequences of an action determine its morality. There are two different kinds of utilitarianism, one which puts an emphasis on the consequences for the individual concerned, the other on the good of society or the greatest number of people. Prof. Jones argued both positions. He was not guided by any ethical principles other than what good results from actions. One form of this philosophy that is very widespread today is known as hedonism. Hedonism holds that something is good if I get pleasure out of it; something is bad if I get no pleasure out of it. Thus, the hedonist would say abortion is OK for a mother if having the baby would cause her too much distress. The hedonist also follows the Playboy philosophy of life. The playboy or playgirl would say pre-marital sex, for example, is OK if you can avoid pain (like an un-wanted pregnancy or venereal disease) and get a lot of pleasure out of the act. Much of modern-day advertising is hedonistic. It tells us to indulge, to seek pleasure for the sake of pleasure, to do something because it feels good.

This philosophy is contrary to Catholic morality. There is more to morality than considering the consequences of our actions. We have already seen the importance of intentions and how the action itself communicates something about the human thing to do. The human is not merely a pleasure-seeking animal going after his or her own self-interest. The child of God is interested in the rights of others, both the individual and the larger community. He identifies with Jesus' call to service and sacrifice for others and is firmly committed to care for the "least of these" (perhaps, in today's world, this would refer to helpless human life).

2. *Ms. Smith.* Smith represents a philosophy of extreme individualism. This philosophy puts so much stress on individual self-fulfillment that others are often ignored. Her argument that the woman has an absolute right to her own body reflects this bias. The Christian maintains that an individual person is a being with and for others. Our bodies and lives are involved with the lives and bodies of others. They are God-given gifts which we are free to control and use responsibly. But responsible use means that we must respect the lives and bodies of others.

This philosophy has many modern manifestations. For example, there are many psychological self-help therapies that concentrate on individual self-fulfillment. To a degree, these can be good, but many of them advocate concentrating on the individual to the exclusion of others. People can get so wrapped up in their own problems and concerns that they soon forget the concerns and problems of others. Overindulgence of self is another brand of hedonism. The Christian reminds himself or herself of the little saying that goes like this: "I felt sorry for myself for not owning any shoes until I saw a person who had no feet." Because we are social beings, our morality can never solely rest on the individual's wants and desires.

3. *Mr. Johnson.* Johnson represents the philosophical approach outlined in the STOP sign. His arguments were those of a Catholic Christian who is concerned about protecting innocent life.

4. *Sarah Williams.* Williams represents an atheistic philosophy. An atheist does not believe in God. Thus, all appeals to religion and values that go beyond a person's immediate experience are excluded from consideration. Her particular form of atheism as described above reflects a social Darwinism. This philosophy holds that human evolution dictates the survival of the fittest. Virtues such as love and concern for others do not fit this mold. Again, there are two forms of this—one which puts an emphasis on the individual and another on the group. Ms. Williams put the emphasis on the individual. A communist would tend to emphasize

the group over the individual. What is necessary for the group to survive is what is good for the individual. Thus, abortion would be OK according to a communist if it is good for group survival such as in the case of overpopulation.

The Christian position recognizes the importance of the community but not at the expense of the individual who has certain inalienable rights, one of which is the right to life.

These descriptions are necessarily sketchy and brief but they do point out some of the conflicting starting points people bring to moral problems like abortion. Try to empathize with them a bit and do the following two exercises.

Case 1: Here is a recent case which was widely reported in the newspapers. It is another "lifeboat ethics" case. An uncle and his nephew were trying to sail their boat a marathon distance. They were to be at sea a number of days. In the middle of their journey, the boat capsized. They spent hours trying to turn it over. They succeeded but they only managed to save a little fresh water from their provisions. The uncle decided that it was not enough water for both of them to make it to land. He scrawled a message to his family on a tin can telling them that he was sorry and that he loved them. He jumped over the side against the protests of his teenage nephew. The uncle said it was better that one of them had a chance to live; both of them could not make it. A couple of days later the young man was rescued. He told the story of his heroic uncle. Below are listed a number of statements about this case. Try to decide which of our four characters involved in the abortion debate would say what.

—— The uncle was a hero. No greater love has a man than he give up his life for another.

—— The uncle was a fool. He should have watched out for his own self-interest and tried to throw his nephew overboard.

—— Whether the uncle was right or not depends on which of the two could have been more useful to the most people involved. He had a family and a good job. As a result, he probably was of more value than his nephew who was not married. Therefore, he did the wrong thing.

—— They should have drawn lots. Let chance determine their fate. If neither wanted to go, as intelligent beings they should have been allowed to die together. What the uncle did was stupid as they both had an equal right to live.

Case 2: Write a little dialogue among our four characters debating the following moral issue: "Whether the United States government should cut back its defense budget by one billion dollars and use the money to aid the poor in hunger programs."

ABORTION RECONSIDERED

The following section will discuss a few thoughts on the topic of abortion. You are encouraged to discuss this moral issue in light of the STOP sign. A bibliography at the end of the chapter may prove helpful in researching the topic, but first consider the few ideas discussed in this section.

Why the controversy? In our country, the controversy on abortion reached a critical point in January, 1973, when the Supreme Court handed down its landmark decision, *Roe v. Wade*. The Court ruled that no law could be made concerning abortion in the first three months of pregnancy. In the second three months, laws could be made only for the sake of the health of the mother. Only in the last three months are states allowed to make laws to protect the fetus, but abortion must still be permitted to save the life and health of the mother. That decision opened the flooddikes. Although people illegally procured abortions before 1973, after that date abortion clinics opened around the country to an alarming degree. Abortion has reached such proportions that it is conservatively estimated that more babies are aborted than born in Washington, D.C.

The Catholic teaching on abortion is quite clear. The *Pastoral Constitution on the Church in the Modern World* reaffirmed the church's constant teaching when it said: "Therefore, from the moment of its conception life must be guarded with the greatest care, while abortion and infanticide are unspeakable crimes." The basis of the church's teaching hinges on several principles. First, we assume that from the moment of conception, a fertilized ovum (zygote) is human life, a developing human person. Second, we believe that all humans are deserving of respect because they are God's creatures with the dignity of being called his children. No one has to earn this respect by what he or she does. A person deserves it by virtue of his or her very existence. Third, we attempt to follow Jesus' mandate to care "for the least of these." In a special way, our love and concern should reach out and encompass those who are unable to care for themselves. Old and sick people, the poor, a developing human, retarded children and other helpless individuals especially need our love and support.

Many, many people in our society accept abortion. Why? A number of them do not accept the fact that an embryo (a developing child before eight weeks) or a fetus (the term used to describe the baby after eight weeks) is actually what we call human life. They argue that a fetus becomes human at some point or other (people vary on just when this takes place) and that before that time (whenever it might be) an abortion should be seen as any other surgical operation. Others argue that a person is not really human until he or she can relate to others in an intelligent way. This latter definition of what it means to be human is very troublesome because it excludes hopelessly senile adults, the retarded, infants before a year or so, and even you when you are sleeping.

From the scientific point of view, we can prove with certainty that human life begins at conception. We have already seen that the zygote has the complete genetic package of a human. At 10 days, the first veins are developing. Between 18 and 25 days, the heart is beating and pumping blood. It goes on from there. The presumption must be in favor of this developing human life; it deserves protection.

Others who accept abortion use arguments like those made by our characters in the debate. Some admit that there is human life but that it does not deserve or need our respect. The rights of the living outside the womb are more important. To this we answer: every person created by God has an equal right to live. The right to live is not something that has to be earned.

What are some of the effects of abortion? For the child, abortion means death. This is a rather final verdict. For the mother, there can be a host of physical complications like infection, hemorrhage, perforation of the uterus or laceration of the cervix. In subsequent pregnancies there can be premature labor and delivery, tubal pregnancies, sterility, miscarriage and an increase in infant deaths from congenital malformations. In some women there are grave psychological complications bringing about neuroses and psychoses. For society in general, there is the loss of incalculably valuable human life, humans who might have grown into the greatest of men and women. There is a general lack of respect for life that pervades society and colors all that it does. Tolerance for a lack of respect at the beginning of human life may very well lead to a lack of care for life in its golden years or at any point in between, wherever humans are not seen as useful.

Besides the effects mentioned above, a more subtle effect should be pointed out here. The current legal toleration of unlimited abortions encourages a lack of accountability. Society is taught and even encouraged to think that if a couple made a "mistake" and had an unplanned conception, they need have no worry or accountability; they can easily "get out of it." Such an attitude mocks personal responsibility and in the last analysis enslaves people who are unwilling to accept the consequences of their actions. Mature persons are willing to admit their mistakes and sins and answer for them. Only immature people seek to take the "easy way out" even if that way compounds the initial mistake a hundredfold. Morality deals with responsibility, the state of being answerable for one's deeds.

To Think About:

Hippocratic oath includes: "I will not give to a woman an instrument to produce abortion."

What would you do? Norman St. John-Stevas once told this story: A doctor asked his colleague for his opinion about the following case: "The father was syphilitic and the mother tubercular. Four children had already been born. The first was blind; the second died; the third was deaf and dumb; and the fourth was tubercular. What would you have done?" His colleague replied, "I would have terminated the pregnancy." "Then," he said, "you would have killed Beethoven." [Cited by Fr. John F. Dedek, *Human Life: Some Moral Issues* (New York: Sheed and Ward, 1972), p. 173.]

Catholic attitude to pluralism. Practically speaking, what can be done about this moral issue? Many people in our society criticize rather severely some of the steps Catholics and pro-lifers in other denominations have taken to reverse the Supreme Court decision, steps such as a constitutional pro-life amendment. They claim we are forcing our morality on them. This is a claim we can reject. We need not be afraid to take steps to protect what we believe is innocent life. It is our right as citizens and our duty as followers of Jesus to protect the helpless, those who cannot defend themselves from unjust attacks on their lives. We in the Catholic community should be proud of whatever efforts we take in fighting the widespread abortion mentality in our country. We admit that we live in a pluralistic society. We cannot help but be affected by the views of others. We have a duty to listen to and try to understand their views. But we need not follow the majority and, in fact, when the majority is wrong, we must take positive steps to correct it. Over and above this, here are some practical guidelines for a person who wishes to get involved in this issue:

1. Know church teaching.

In its simplest form, the church condemns a direct attack on the life of another. In almost every case, abortion is a direct attack on human life, equivalent to unjustified killing. The church is not heartless in her teaching, though. Under grave circumstances she allows an indirect abortion. For example, if a fetus dies as a result of a life-saving operation on the mother (for example, operating on a cancerous uterus), then the operation is permissible if the operation is a last resort; the fetus is not directly attacked and the intention is to save life, not take it. This exception is known as the principle of the double effect. This principle operates when a good or neutral action (such as an operation on cancer) results in two effects: one good (the saving of the mother's life) and one evil (the foreseen but *unintended* death of the fetus.) This principle can only be invoked when the action is absolutely necessary, when the good effect is willed (the evil only permitted), and the means used are not evil.

2. Fight for what you believe is right but be slow to condemn others.

It is very difficult to see how reasonable men and women believe that a fetus from the moment of its conception cannot be human life. Some honestly do not see it our way. They permit abortion. We think they are objectively wrong, but we must be slow to judge them. Terms like "murderers" should be reserved for God's judgment. These terms bring more heat than light to the debate. Rather, we should fight for those changes in the law that will protect the lives of the unborn that we so cherish. By prayer and good, hard knowledge of the facts, we, as members of a Catholic community, should try to change people's hearts to see the enormity of what is taking place.

3. We must educate others.

We educate not only by discussing and debating the topic, that is, letting our views be known, but also by the way we live. Respecting all life is a way to show others that we mean business when it comes to fetal life. The way we drive our cars, our concern for the poor and the outcast, our stand on capital punishment and war—all communicate very powerfully what we mean when we talk about life and the respect due it.

4. As a Catholic community, we must show care, concern and love for those threatened.

In this, the church's record has been outstanding. Orphanages, hospitals, homes for the aged, the Bishops' Relief Fund, Catholic Charities—all of these speak very loudly about our concern for the helpless and hurt in society. We must continue our fine record here. Furthermore, we must work for a reform in the very structures of society that tend to discriminate against the poor, weak, helpless, minorities and the like. We must be advocates for the poor. We must let it be known that we will lend moral, physical, psychological and financial help to any woman who brings her child into the world. In addition, we should stand ready, if necessary, to help that mother and child in the difficult years after birth. This latter suggestion will test our true sincerity. It is one thing to encourage a person to have the child, it is another to be willing to help in raising the child. Unless we are willing to do that as a Christian community, our stand on abortion will not be believed.

An Action Project

As a group, devise some project that will do two things:

1. Let your stand on the prolife issue be known. (Examples like writing letters to newspapers, legislators, etc.)

2. Raise money to help an organization like Birthright. Perhaps the fund-raising can be organized in a way to let people know why you are raising the money.

Exercise:

A high school friend tells you that she is contemplating getting an abortion. In light of the STOP sign, what would you tell her?

Discussion:

Name and discuss the projects or operations of your own diocese which relate to protecting and helping life.

SUMMARY

1. We live in a pluralistic society with many views of morality. The issue of abortion points out this pluralism in a stark manner.

2. Utilitarianism judges right and wrong in light of the effects alone, either for the individual or the group.

3. Hedonism holds that something is good if it brings pleasure; it is evil if it causes pain.

4. Extreme individualism makes each person the center of moral judgment. Others are ignored in the moral analysis.

5. Atheism refuses to accept any religious arguments in making moral judgments. One brand of atheism is social-Darwinism which claims that only the fittest deserve to survive.

6. The Catholic Church stands for life by categorically rejecting all direct attacks on human life, including abortion.

7. Church teaching rests on the principles of the dignity of each human life as creature and child of God and the protection of the helpless from the moment of conception (at which point human life begins).

8. Catholics and other pro-lifers need not be afraid to assert their values in a pluralistic society. Civil law can be immoral; the majority can be wrong.

9. Prayer, education, respect for life in all its forms, care and concern for those threatened and knowledge of the facts are positive ways to get involved actively in the abortion issue.

Bibliography on Abortion

Callahan, Daniel. *Abortion: Law, Choice and Morality.* New York: Doubleday, 1970. A classic in the field, but some difficult reading.

Connery, John. S. J. *Abortion: The Development of the Roman Catholic Perspective.* Chicago: Loyola University Press, 1977. Fr. Connery traces the development of the Roman Catholic attitude toward abortion from the beginning of the Christian era to contemporary times.

Cooke, Robert E., ed. *The Terrible Choice: The Abortion Dilemma.* New York: Bantam, 1968. Some excellent chapters.

Critelli, Ida and Tom Schick. *Unmarried and Pregnant: What Now?* Cincinnati: St. Anthony Messenger Press, 1977. This book is intended to help the young, unmarried, pregnant woman deal with the problems and decisions she will face.

Grisez, Germain G. *Abortion: The Myths, the Realities, and the Arguments.* New York: Corpus, 1970. Highly recommended. Cogent writing from an important Catholic theologian.

Hilgers, Dr. Thomas W. and Dr. Robert P. Shearin. *Induced Abortion: A Documented Report.* Minneapolis: Minnesota Citizens Concerned for Life, 1973. Has an excellent chapter on alternatives to abortion.

Joyce, Robert and Mary. *Let Us Be Born.* Chicago: Franciscan Herald Press, 1971. A sensitive, easy-to-read book.

Kramer, HM, Sister Rose Marie and Sister Karen Walsh, HM. *God Loves Life! A Christian Approach to Human Life Issues.* New York: William H. Sadlier, Inc., 1978. An excellent resource written primarily for high school students.

The National Right to Life Committee. Box 9365, Washington, D.C. 20005. Write for resources.

Noonan, John T. *The Morality of Abortion: Legal and Historical Perspectives.* Cambridge, Mass.: Harvard University Press, 1970. Along with Callahan's work, this is one of the important books in the field.

Respect Life. Committee for Pro-Life Activities, National Conference of Catholic Bishops. 1312 Massachusetts Ave., NW, Washington, D.C. 20005, 1977-1978. An excellent resource guide on pro-life issues. It cites church teaching and gives many fine resources.

Wakin, Edward. *Helping the Unwed Mother.* Chicago: Claretian Publications, 1975. Contains useful information about, and services for, the unmarried mother.

Willke, Dr. and Mrs. J. C. *Handbook on Abortion.* Cincinnati: Hiltz Publishing Co., 1973. An important and widely read book by national leaders in the right to life movement.

7

Morality and Sin

If we say, "We are free of the guilt of sin,"
we deceive ourselves; the truth is not to be found in us.
But if we acknowledge our sins,
he who is just can be trusted
to forgive our sins
and cleanse us from every wrong.
If we say, "We have never sinned,"
we make him a liar
and his word finds no place in us.

                                        (1 John 1:8-10)

Few love to hear the sins they love to act.
                        —William Shakespeare

A discussion of sin has its place in a larger treatment on how to resolve moral problems. Knowing all the right questions to ask about a moral issue does not guarantee that we will do the right thing. Sin is a reality that is much larger than making mistakes. The great St. Paul knew this better than anyone when he said: "I cannot even understand my own actions. I do not do what I want to do but what I hate. . . . What happens is that I do, not the good I will to do, but the evil I do not intend" (Rom 7:15, 19). St. Paul attributes his inability to do the right thing, even though he knows it is right, to the reality known as sin. How often have you been victim to the same web of evil in which St. Paul found himself? For example, you resolved never to mock out a classmate again, but soon found yourself doing it. You promised to avoid an occasion which led you into a sexual sin, but weakness set in and you fell again. You made a firm resolve to study for a difficult math exam, but temptation came along and once again you gave in to distractions. If you experienced any of the above or similar expressions of weakness, you know firsthand about the reality of sin.

A sense of sin adds the element of reality to a discussion of morality. It brings us back to earth and helps us to see that morality is more than just knowing the right thing to do. Being a good person means following through on our knowledge, it means consistency in being who we are. But we are inconsistent; we falter at times; we sin. To deny the reality of sin in our lives or in society as a whole is to be unrealistic. A sense of sin recognizes that people's cruelty to their fellow humans rests in their ability to destroy, to hate, to turn from the good. Examples of this abound in our world. Racism, sexism, misuse of the world's goods, failure to help the hungry, murders, rape, and cheating are just the tip of the iceberg of the pervasive reality known as sin.

This chapter will attempt to look more closely at this reality which keeps us from doing the right thing. Before the discussion proceeds, take this little survey on sin. Below are some statements which reflect attitudes about the reality of sin. Check on the scale whether what is being said reflects an escape from accepting sin as a reality (1) or is a truthful statement about the real nature of sin (5). The numbers in between represent different degrees of agreement or disagreement with these two polarities.

Survey on attitudes to sin:

1. I'm doing right if I don't hurt anyone.

2. Something is a sin merely because the church says it is.

3. Sin is more what I think than what I do.

4. Sin is more tied into my actions than my attitudes.

    1   2   3   4   5

5. Sin is too old-fashioned an idea for contemporary men and women.

    1   2   3   4   5

6. Sin is something personal—between me and God.

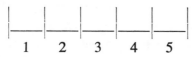

    1   2   3   4   5

7. In essence, sin is a failure to grow in relationship to God and others.

    1   2   3   4   5

8. No one has the right to tell me that I might be sinning.

    1   2   3   4   5

9. Another name for sin is "mistakes of judgment."

    1   2   3   4   5

10. If a person doesn't think that he or she has sinned, then there is no sin.

    1   2   3   4   5

TALK OF SIN

Over the ages, theologians have identified the so-called "capital sins." These sins are called "capital" because from them flow many other kinds of wrongdoing. They are: pride, covetousness, lust, anger, gluttony, envy and sloth. This catalogue of key sins brings us to the two most common ways of talking about sin in the scriptures. In both the Old and New Testaments, sin is seen as "missing the mark" and "hardness of heart." To miss the mark means primarily to fail to conform to the covenant relationship God has established between himself and his people. The Jews did this when they worshiped the golden calf, that is, when they put their loyalty in something other than their source of life, Lord God (Dt 9:16). They failed to love their God, and then substituted a false god. They missed the mark, the target if you will, of their response to God's invitation to love. He promised to be faithful to them; they were to respond in kind. God's loving kindness to his people is always there for his children to respond to; sin is a failure to respond to that love.

Love is often associated with the image of the heart. This is why a failure to love was often depicted as a cold or hard heart on the part of the sinner. Note the image used by Jeremiah when he called his people to repent of their sins: "Cleanse your heart of evil, O Jerusalem, that you may be saved" (Jer 4:14). Jesus himself disclosed sin in the depths of a person's heart when he said:

> What emerges from within a man, that and nothing else is what makes him impure. Wicked designs come from the deep recesses of the heart: acts of fornication, theft, murder, adulterous conduct, greed, maliciousness, deceit, sensuality, envy, blasphemy, arrogance, an obtuse spirit. All these evils come from within and render a man impure (Mk 7:20-23).

In the last analysis, then, all sin is an unwillingness to open ourselves to God's love and carrying it to others and ourselves. Sin is the refusal to love God, to love others, or to love one's self. God's covenant of love is an invitation to be his children, an invitation that merits us eternal life. To accept the invitation means to love our Father above all things and to love our neighbor as ourselves. Sin, ultimately, is saying "no" to the invitation of love. When a person sins, he or she substitutes something else for the love of God. His or her heart is frozen in a kind of self-love which puts the self before God and others. The sin of pride illustrates this very well. The target of pride is self; the heart is frozen in on pursuit of its own self-interest to the exclusion of God and others. A person who is unwilling to listen to the advice of others, for example, is saying that "I don't need anyone else. I can go it alone. I don't need your help, or your love. I'm self-sufficient." This is the great lie of sin— it cuts the ties of relationship we have with God and others. It is a distortion of love which refuses to reach out and embrace the other.

Omission and commission. Hardness of heart and missing the true mark take the form of two kinds of sinful postures: inaction and action. We often forget about the first, that is, the sins of omission. Jesus, however, often pointed to examples of self-cen-teredness which were primarily sins of a cold heart, sins of apathy. For example, his picture of the Last Judgment is that those who condemn themselves to hell are those who failed to feed the hungry, clothe the naked, visit the sick and the like (Mt 25:41-46). The sinners in the parable of the Good Samaritan were those who failed to come to the aid of the bleeding victim. He also condemned the Pharisees for not keeping the higher demands of love, namely, justice, mercy and good faith despite their doing all the "right things" according to their law. We, too, sin by omission when we fail to get involved—to speak out for the truth, to defend the help-less (in the abortion issue, for example), to befriend the lonely classmate, to be concerned about the poor, to let others make decisions for us. Apathy is another word for omission; responsi-bility is its opposite. The capital sin of sloth (laziness) is apathy dressed in its most glaring clothes. Slothfulness appears when a person refuses to pray, refuses to learn, and refuses to risk helping another.

Sins of commission are easier to catalogue because they are easier to see. They most often take place when we fail to treat others as we would like to be treated. They take place when we treat the other not as a subject like ourselves but as an object. For example, people are sometimes the most cruel when they get behind the wheel of a car. They sometimes treat other drivers and pedestrians as things in their way and react in ways that often endanger life. Sexual sins are also committed because others are seen not as persons to be loved and cherished for their individuality but as objects for our own self-gratification. When we steal, we treat another as a thing, not a person. When we gossip about others we are really being insensitive to the feelings of a person, we are treating the individual as a nonperson. The list could go on and on.

From this discussion of sin as a failure to love, as a failure to respond to God's invitation to friendship, it is clear that all sin is social. Sin never just involves me. For example, when I fail to worry about overconsumption of food (gluttony), I am failing to share the goods of the world to which others are entitled. They are hurt by this, whether I care to admit it or not. Population experts conservatively predict that two persons per minute die of starvation each day. Not responding to this reality is contributing to the problem. Others are affected by what I do—and don't do. Even my private thoughts of prejudicial hate and revenge have their social manifestations. They color the way I will act to all people I meet. They will tend to close me off, make me more self-centered and less loving.

Discussing sin from a biblical perspective reveals that it is missing the mark of true love of God and neighbor. Sin is also coldness of heart which always affects others, either by what I do or fail to do.

Exercises:

Capital sins: Give an example of each of the following capital sins. Briefly discuss how this example is a failure to love, a true missing of the mark and coldheartedness.

Sin	Example	Discussion
Pride		
Covetousness		
Lust		
Anger		
Gluttony		
Envy		
Sloth		

Sin is more like . . . : In light of what you just read, choose which option seems to be more "coldhearted."

   ——— Cheating on an exam

   ——— Failing to help a friend study for an exam

   ——— Joining a club which keeps out blacks

   ——— Refusing to work against neighborhood segregation (your neighborhood)

   ——— Refusing to go to Mass

   ——— Verbally abusing those who do go to Mass

   ——— Revealing personal secrets entrusted to you by a friend

   ——— Failing to tell your parents the truth about why you were out late

   ——— Claiming there is nothing you can do about the hunger problem

   ——— Spending $5 on junk food

Discuss:

Identify the sins of omission. What makes one sin worse than another?

SINNING: Saying "No"

Some people do not like to talk about sin because they have a horrible image of a God ready to "zap" it to anyone who falls into mortal sin. The picture they have in mind goes something like this: There is a basically good person who has lived a good life. On one occasion, he or she makes the fatal mistake of committing a mortal sin. Unfortunately, death comes before the person can repent of the sin. The all-just God (notice his justice, not his mercy, is emphasized) judges the sinner and condemns him or her to hell. The end of the story.

What a terrible way to image both sin and God! First of all, the idea that God is "out to get us" the first moment we slip up is a real distortion of the loving Abba (daddy) whom Jesus pictures in the New Testament. God is not some coldhearted, stern taskmaster who loves to send his creatures to hell. As a matter of fact, the good news of salvation is that the Father already has us in a loving, intimate relationship sealed in friendship by his Son Jesus. God's wish is that we keep saying "yes" to this relationship by responding in love to him and our neighbor. His judgment of us will be our own judgment. Our judgment will consist of our basic direction of life, that is, whether we have been for God and others or turned in on ourselves. Our judgment will consist of the basic story of our lives, not of an isolated word or sentence.

The trouble with the distorted picture of sin that some people have been taught is that they picture sin as being somehow removed from the overall direction of one's life. If one's basic attitude toward God is one of friendship and love, then one will basically act in accord with that attitude. Sure, as in all friendships, there might be moments of hesitation, even steps backward. But if one is striving to get closer to a friend, the overall tendency of the relationship will be toward the good. This basic choice for friendship, and living in accordance with it, will be what we are judged on. Likewise, if one's basic attitude is a turning toward self, then the acts which flow from the relationship will tend to be hardhearted ones that fail to take into consideration God and others. A pattern of self-centered thoughts and acts can harden into a pattern where one can say there is no relationship—it is dead. At judgment time, a person will not even recognize or want to be with the Lord because all he or she has seen and worked for in life was self. And self is what one will get in the afterlife. This, of course, is another name for hell. In his marvelous fantasy about hell, entitled *The Great Divorce,* the great English author C. S. Lewis describes hell in precisely these terms. People in hell do not even want to be with others (this is heaven) because they are self-satisfied in their own desperate and lonely isolation.

So, in clearing up the distortion about sin and judgment, we should note that our judgment consists of the overall quality and direction of our lives. We are not judged on a single mistake but on whether we can say that our basic stance is for God and others or inward toward ourselves. Within this framework, then, we can talk about the different kinds of sin. Traditionally, theologians have talked about mortal sin and venial sin, though today many of them add a third category—serious sin. Let us discuss each of them briefly.

Mortal sin. Mortal sin is deadly, or fatal sin. It kills the friendship between God and man. It is not entered into lightly. It is certainly not easy for a person whose basic stance in life is for God and others to kill that relationship by a single isolated indiscreet action. The church has recognized the seriousness of this point by saying a person can kill a relationship only if three conditions are fulfilled:

> 1) *The action or omission is seriously wrong.* For example, murder is terrible action that kills friendship and a relationship (rather permanently, at that). Other serious acts would include rape, adultery, discrimination in all its ugly forms, blasphemy, gross misuse of the goods God gave us, like sex, our bodies, the riches of the world, etc. Theologians call this "grave matter," and it includes whatever deeply affects us in our relationships to God and others.

2) *The person knows that what he or she is doing is wrong.* Just as a person cannot be held accountable for laws he or she could not reasonably be expected to know, so, too, persons cannot be accused of mortal sin if, through no fault of their own, they do not know that what they are doing is seriously wrong. Of course, the mature person with a developing conscience will always be open to new data which will help him or her see more clearly what helps love grow or what diminishes or kills relationships. To be so closed as not to allow new information is itself seriously wrong.

3) *Full consent of the will is given.* To sin fatally, a person must freely choose to turn from God, to reject his love and invitation to friendship. Modern psychology shows that there are many impediments that destroy or weaken this kind of freedom, impediments such as fear, passion and habit. For example, a person might commit a sexual sin which he or she did not fully intend. The passion of the moment carried along the person involved. This lessens responsibility, but a person has an obligation, then, to avoid those occasions which give rise to that kind of passion. Furthermore, psychology shows that the human person is capable of freely and willfully making a decision that represents a deathblow in a relationship. This would be an example of "full consent." A coolly calculated and willful act of hate or exploitation (again, for example, a sexual sin) is a real possibility for a human.

For a person who has continually lived in friendship, it is not easy to fulfill these three conditions. If friendship with the Lord is something we work at continuously, killing that friendship is something we work at, too. For a friendship to die, we normally begin by neglecting it. We start out by ignoring the other, by letting little distractions and indiscretions enter the relationship until we deliver the fatal blow that kills the relationship or until the relationship just does not exist any longer. To say that it is difficult to kill a loving relationship with one fell swoop (one mortal sin) does not mean it is impossible to do so. People can and sometimes do act defiantly in a single act of rebellion which is so serious that friendship is killed.

Serious Sin. Serious sin, then, refers to acts or attitudes we harbor that look like they are seriously wrong and could kill the relationship. But we just do not know if for a given individual they actually do kill the relationship. Sometimes they might; at other times they do not. We can only conjecture. At the least, they rock the relationship to its very foundation. They involve serious matter but perhaps do not represent for the individual a clear break from his or her basic option of choosing for God and others. Ordinarily, full consent of the will was not given in the action.

Venial sin. Venial sin is not-yet-fatal sinfulness. It does not represent a "no" in the relationship. It consists of light matter which does not cut at the heart of the relationship. Whereas mortal sin is an outright refusal of God's friendship which alienates a person from God, others and self, venial sin can often be pictured as a refusal to grow, a sidestepping of the relationship. It is something to be concerned about. It is a detour in the relationship. It can lead to a progressive kind of deterioration in the relationship, a lukewarmness. Failing to pray, to admit wrong, to cooperate, being sarcastic, mistrustful, trying to dominate others, lying—all are examples of venial sin. A common but unhealthy attitude people have is "It's only a venial sin." But people who are in love never say, for example, "I only mocked you out" or "It was just a small lie." Friends are concerned and try to eradicate anything from a relationship that hurts it. Furthermore, venial sin can lead to an attitude of lukewarmness that makes it possible to harden one's heart so much that one might be willing to turn completely away from God, that is, sin mortally. A husband, for example, does not normally just go out one day and commit adultery (a mortal sin). His act of infidelity is usually preceded by small infidelities, neglect, lack of love and the like before the drastic act of adultery.

Real sin is self-centeredness. Sin makes the person the center of reality. Sin is hedging on one's total surrender to God and others, on loving with one's whole being. Sin is a rejection of personal responsibility. It is a failure to grow. It is a failure to do the good that is called for in a relationship. It is denying the dictates of my conscience out of fear, laziness, pride or whatever. Sin is unwillingness to take the risks of sharing my talents, of doing the good that I know might bring criticism from others. In essence, sin is *not* doing what I ought to do to grow in love; it is a failure to respond to God and others.

For Reflection:

1. *What's your conception of God?* From the following list, check those attributes which truly represent the Abba of the New Testament. As a class, try to find an example from scripture to support your choices.

—— stern	—— loving
—— fair	—— sympathetic
—— happy	—— old
—— punishing	—— pitying
—— lenient	—— removed
—— demanding	—— vengeful
—— angry	—— forgiving
—— compassionate	—— concerned
—— merciful	—— cold
—— emotionless	—— faithful
—— overbearing	—— friendly

Regarding the items you did not check, why do you think some people might feel God is this way?

Can you add some traits of your own to this list?

2. *Serious matter.* Check any of the following which you think have a tendency to kill friendship, that is, constitute "grave matter." Give a reason why this represents a killing kind of action or attitude.

Act/attitude	Reasons
—— failing to care for old people	
—— smoking joints	
—— consistently not going to Mass on Sunday	
—— being sarcastic	
—— failing to befriend a lonely classmate	
—— fearing the opposite sex	
—— rich nations exploiting the natural resources of poor nations	
—— reading pornographic literature	
—— committing adultery	
—— revealing that a person known to you is a homosexual	
—— disobeying traffic laws	

3. *Am I sinning or not?* The great Protestant preacher Dr. Harry Emerson Fosdick gave the following six-point test for deciding right from wrong. You might find his list helpful, even though he fails to mention prayer as an essential ingredient in the process of choosing the right thing to do. Here is his list:

- Does what you propose to do sound reasonable? Forget what others have to say. Does it make sense to you—if so it is probably right.

- Is it sporting, that is, if everyone did the same thing would it benefit all?

- Where will your action lead? In other words, how will it affect others? What will it do to you?

- Will you have good thoughts about yourself when you look back over what you have done?

- Separate yourself from the problem. Imagine that the problem belongs to the person you most admire. Ask yourself how that person would treat the problem.

- Hold your final decision up to the glaring light of publicity. Would you want your family and friends to know what you have done? The decisions we make hoping that no one will find out about them are usually wrong.

Discussion:

Remember how Adam tried to blame his sin on Eve and Eve tried to put the blame on the snake? This is the classic example of a failure to accept responsibility. Why do people try to rationalize (that is, make excuses for) their sins? How is this a failure to grow?

JESUS AND FORGIVENESS

Let us return to St. Paul. He expressed better than anyone the reality of sin as a pervasive force in our lives. The good we want to do we do not do; the evil we wish to avoid, we do not avoid. This propensity to do the wrong thing, even when knowing the right thing, is a part of the human condition. It is an effect of original sin. An adequate definition of the human person must take into account that we are sinners, capable of doing grave harm to ourselves and others. Philosophies which deny this aspect of our person are fundamentally unrealistic. They fail to take into account all the data about the human person. Christians believe that this tendency to sin, this inability to choose the right, results from original sin. We cannot, on our own merits, overcome this condition.

Christian faith maintains that Jesus has overcome sin and its major effect—death. The great Paschal Mystery of the suffering-death-resurrection-ascension of Jesus attests to the fact that through

Jesus sin has been conquered. Our Lord Jesus has the power to help us overcome our sin, our weakness and our tendency to choose the wrong. This is why prayer is so important to choosing the right. Our Lord's power and his Spirit can give us the strength to choose what we ought to choose even when our inclinations take us in the opposite direction.

Furthermore, the Catholic believes that Jesus left his power of forgiving and healing sin with his church. In the sacrament of Reconciliation, the sacrament of peace, the Christian can receive Christ's forgiveness. There is something psychologically sound about receiving a concrete sign of God's forgiveness in a context where we become reconciled to the community. Also, confessing our sins helps us to admit what is keeping us from growth. Articulating our sins helps us see for ourselves where the problem areas are in our lives and enables the divine physician to get at the root causes of our alienation.

The recently revised Rite of Reconciliation in the church presents Jesus not as a stern judge of our actions but as a brother who takes us to his forgiving, loving Father. The sacrament brings God's love and forgiveness to the individual in a context of communal support and friendship. It is a powerful sign that what we do affects not only ourselves, but others as well, and that our road to cementing and growing in a loving relationship needs the strength and support of our loving Father and our fellow believers.

Catholics who regularly avail themselves of the sacrament of Reconciliation often see great signs of growth. The graces of the sacrament help them honestly confront themselves in an attempt to lead a life of response to God and others. For the Catholic, then, the sacrament of peace is a profound help in living a moral life, of rooting out the symptoms of a self-centered life. Anyone serious about doing the right thing will certainly consider using this wonderful occasion of growth toward holiness.

SUMMARY

1. Sin is a reality in our lives which keeps us from doing what we ought to do as persons growing in friendship with God and neighbor.

2. Biblical images of sin include the notion of missing the target and coldheartedness.

3. Sins of omission are failures to respond to God and neighbor; sins of commission are acts which distort our true relationship with others.

4. The quality of our lives, our general direction either toward God and neighbor or away from them, determines our ultimate judgment.

5. Mortal sin consists of a fatal blow to a loving relationship with God and neighbor. It is not entered into lightly. To sin mortally, there must be grave matter, knowledge of the wrongdoing and full consent of the will.

6. Serious sin involves grave matter and can rock a relationship to its very foundation. Full consent of the will is not usually present in serious sin.

7. Venial sin is a lukewarmness in our covenant-love relationship with God and neighbor. It involves light matter but is something to be concerned about because it does not contribute anything to the relationship of love and friendship.

8. To deny that we are sinners is to look at the human condition unrealistically.

9. The Christian believes that only Jesus can conquer sin. For the Catholic, prayer and the sacrament of peace are both necessary and powerful helps in living a moral life.

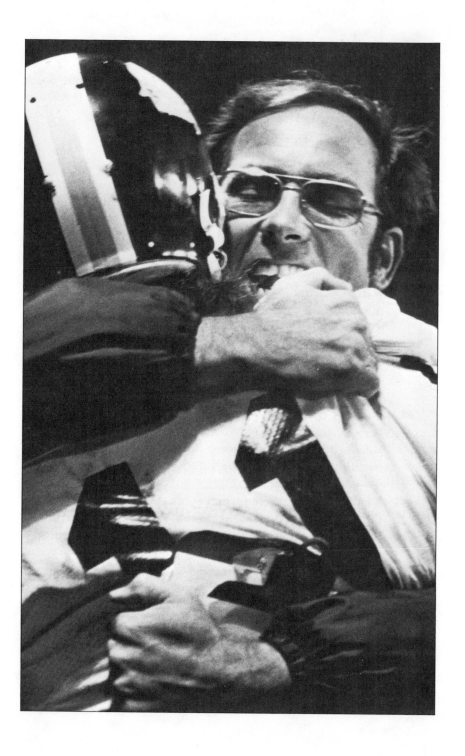

8

Solving Moral Problems: What About Life?

Every man's life is a plan of God.
    —Horace Bushnell

I count all that part of my life lost which I spent not in communion with God, or in doing good.
    —John Donne

This chapter, along with the next two, presents a number of cases for analysis and discussion. The cases will give you an opportunity to apply the method of solving moral problems which you have learned in this book. The present chapter deals with a number of life issues. Life is an extremely important topic in morality because life is at the root of human existence. Life is our greatest gift from God. In an extremely complex society, moral decisions concerning life are often not easy ones to make. Overpopulation, lack of food and health care for all, prolongation of life through sophisticated medical techniques, an escalating arms race, violent crimes, life-styles of ease characterized by an attitude of "doing my own thing"—all of these and more help create serious moral issues dealing with the respect for and preservation of human life.

The Christian attitude to life is preserved in the fifth commandment, "You shall not kill." That prohibition to the taking of life seems quite clear and absolute. The problem is, though, was it ever interpreted that way? Surely, there is a difference be-

177

tween cold-blooded murder and killing in self-defense, between an unjustified attack on another country and fighting to preserve peace, between seeking out and killing "undesirables" in a society (like Hitler did) and putting to death psychopathic killers who are a serious threat to others. In the Old Testament, the commandment simply did *not* prohibit the taking of human life in all circumstances. What the Hebrews did try to do was to instill the value of every human life.

Jesus took the fifth commandment and intensified it. In the Sermon on the Mount, he said:

> You have heard the commandment imposed on your forefathers, "You shall not commit murder; every murderer shall be liable to judgment." What I say to you is: everyone who grows angry with his brother shall be liable to judgment (Mt 5:21-22b).

The heart of Jesus' prohibition was not only to avoid murder but to avoid that which leads to murder. In essence, he called his followers to love. St. John says it best: "The man who does not love is among the living dead. Anyone who hates his brother is a murderer, and you know that eternal life abides in no murderer's heart" (1 Jn 3:14b-15).

The basic value behind this commandment and Jesus' teaching is that God alone is the ultimate Lord and master of life. Life comes from God and belongs to God. As a result, we must respect our own lives and the lives of others. We do not believe that we are the masters of our own lives. Rather, we believe that we are stewards of life. A steward is one who takes care of something for someone else. In the case of life, we watch over all that God has given us—body, soul, spirit, and other people to whom we relate. Our judgments about life should always be made in light of how we are caring for the great gift that God has given us. Our judgments about ourselves and others should be made in light of the basic dignity given to us by God himself, not by what we do, or what we have, or how useful we are. Vatican II taught this truth:

> Coming down to practical and particularly urgent consequences, this council lays stress on reverence for man; everyone must consider his neighbor without exception as another self, taking into account first of all his life and the means necessary of living it with dignity, so as not to imitate the rich man who had no concern for the poor man Lazarus (*Pastoral Constitution on the Church in the Modern World,* No. 27, p. 226).

In light of these general remarks, take an honest stock of yourself on your attitude to life issues by reacting to the following exercise. Give your honest answer to what you really think about the following statements. On the continuum, mark an *X* to represent your degree of agreement or disagreement with the attitude expressed.

HUMAN LIFE INVENTORY:

1. In no circumstance should a young person be asked to go to war for his country.

   Agree————————————————Disagree

2. A terminally ill, long-suffering cancer patient should be put out of his or her misery if he or she requests it.

   Agree————————————————Disagree

3. Guns should be banned.

   Agree————————————————Disagree

4. Rapists, murderers and kidnappers should be put to death to protect society.

   Agree————————————————Disagree

5. Women have the right to terminate a pregnancy.

   Agree————————————————Disagree

6. If scientists develop a pill to help people learn more rapidly, every student should be required to take it.

   Agree————————————————Disagree

7. I would never kill anyone, even in self-defense.

Agree————————————————————Disagree

8. Because of the health hazards involved, cigarette smoking should be banned in public places.

Agree————————————————————Disagree

9. Cloning (asexual reproduction), if perfected by science, should be allowed.

Agree————————————————————Disagree

10. Because of the high number of accidents caused by young people, no one should be allowed to drive until the age of 21.

Agree————————————————————Disagree

11. Much more needs to be done to prevent teenage alcoholism.

Agree————————————————————Disagree

For Discussion:

a. Why did you mark each statement as you did?

b. If you disagreed with a statement, how would you change the sentence to reflect your opinion?

c. Share and discuss your responses with your classmates.

CASES FOR ANALYSIS

The chapter presents four moral cases. In each case you will be asked to decide the morality of the issue discussed. This will give you practice in applying the STOP sign. In thinking through them, you may need more facts about the particular issue. At the end of this chapter, there is an appendix which provides a short bibliography; this can be helpful in digging out some of the facts you need to make a decision on the case. Also, for some of the cases you will find in the appendix a short summary statement or two of the church's official position on the topic or a related issue. You are encouraged to discuss the cases with as many people as possible to help you formulate your decision.

1. Why not hit the car?

Nationally syndicated columnist Mike Royko once told of an amazing true story. One day a young woman was driving on one of Chicago's expressways. She was going rather cautiously as the roads were icy and snow-covered. Out of nowhere, a green car came speeding by and sideswiped her. Her car did a tailspin and came to rest in the path of an onrushing trailer truck. At that moment she thought she was a "goner."

The man driving the semi had one of two choices: continue to go straight, inevitably hitting the woman broadside; cut sharply to the right, risking grave injury to himself and his wife of four months who was in the truck with him.

As he told the story later, he said that he could see that the woman would be killed instantly if he continued on a straight course. Thus, he made a last-second decision to cut right. He hit a light pole, jackknifed sideways and went into a ditch off the side of the road. His brave act resulted in his sustaining several injured vertebrae and a collapsed lung. He had to wear a back brace for nine months; he was unable to go to work. His wife was OK. His truck was demolished.

The woman whose life he saved was extremely grateful.

The kicker to the story is what happened afterwards. The state trooper told him that he would have been better off if he had hit the woman. He would not have wrecked his truck or the light pole and would not have hurt himself. The trooper informed him that he would have been within his rights if he had hit her and that the insurance company would have paid for the damage done.

The people who employed the truck driver also wondered why he did not hit the woman.

The police wrote up the accident report blaming the bad weather since they could not catch the green car which had sped away.

What the truck driver wondered aloud was whether or not he did the right thing in taking the course he did in order to avoid killing the woman. He spent the nine months during recovery thinking about what he did and what the state police and his employers said.

For Discussion:

1. What do you think of this case? Do you admire the truck driver?

2. What do you think about the response of the police and the driver's employer? Is their response typical? Is it realistic?

3. Did the truck driver have the *duty* to cut his wheels? to sacrifice his life? Explain your response.

---

2. Should she quit smoking?

On the basis of overwhelming scientific evidence, the Surgeon General has for a number of years been warning Americans about the real relationship between cigarette smoking and cancer. The link between the two seems so certain that there is a warning printed on cigarette packages: "Cigarette smoking may be hazardous to your health."

A mother knows of this threat. Furthermore, there is a history of cancer in her family. Yet, she persists in her habit of a pack of cigarettes a day. She admits that she is hooked. However, she claims that with three young kids she needs something to calm her nerves. Besides, she enjoys smoking—it helps her to relax. She reasons that when her time comes to die, there is little she can do about it. What will be will be.

Discuss the morality of her habit.

Analysis:

1. Employ the STOP sign to analyze this problem.

    A. *Search:* What?

                Why?

                Who?

                Where?

                When?

                How?

    B. *Think:* Alternatives?

              Consequences?

    C. *Others:* Consulting?

             How affect?

    D. *Pray:*

    E. *Other factors:* Jesus

                    Reason and revelation

                    Imagination

                    Law

                    Church

                    Values

                    Instinct

                    Conscience

2. Would the nature of this habit affect her blameworthiness? Explain.

3. Would she sin if she did not stop smoking? Explain your answer.

4. Can you think of similar cases like this? Discuss them.

5. What if one of the mother's children grew up and, as an 18-year-old, became addicted to heroin? Would this be the same kind of case? Explain.

3. Helping "Gramps" die

Put yourself into this case. "Gramps," a widower for 10 years, is an old man of 78. He has been living with your family for the past five years after developing a severe case of arthritis. He is constantly in pain. Furthermore, he is beginning to feel that he is a burden on your family.

One day you decide to go to his room to try to cheer him up. You notice that he is quite depressed. In talking to him, you learn that he overheard a recent conversation your parents had about the real possibility of putting him in a nursing home. He vows to you that he would rather die than go there. In a very sad voice, he tells you that he is at the end of his life and really wishes he were dead so as not to burden the family any longer. In listening to him you are convinced that he is in such a bad mood that he might even take his own life.

Later, that evening, your parents have gone out to the movies. You did not get a chance to discuss your fears about Gramps with them. You are home alone with him. Suddenly, he loudly calls you to his room. He begs you to get him a glass of water and his sleeping pills. At this point, you are convinced that he is probably going to take an overdose of pills. What would you do?

For Discussion:

1. Using the STOP sign, decide what would be the moral thing for you to do. (You may wish to read the appendix to this chapter for some background information.)

2. Using the STOP sign, decide what would be the moral thing for Gramps to do.

3. *Related questions:*

    a. When a pet is gravely ill or badly wounded, it is often killed to put it out of its pain. Does the same thing apply here? Why or why not?

b. If Gramps were hospitalized, in great pain and with only a few months to live, would the morality of the case change if someone else decided to administer the drug to relieve him of his misery? Explain.

c. Should there be a law preventing doctors (and others, including family members) from administering drugs to hasten someone's death in the case of a terminal illness? Why or why not?

d. You may wish to do research on and discuss the famous Karen Quinlan case.

e. What would you do if the Congress introduced legislation to kill painlessly all old people over the age of 80?

---

4. Kill the killers?

Every few years or so, notorious cases of mass murderers come to the public's attention. The same is true of rapists and heartless kidnappers. Persons like Charles Manson, Richard Speck and, more recently, the "Son of Sam," create a public outcry for revenge. It is at such times that people begin debating the issue of capital punishment, that is, the death penalty for those guilty of heinous crimes.

This is a difficult issue in morality and one that takes much careful thought and argumentation. Divide into groups to research and discuss this issue. Some groups should research and assemble arguments for the "pro" side of the debate; others should do the same for the "con" side.

Below are presented the most common arguments used on both sides of the debate. These positions are only sketched out here to help you get started in sorting out the issues. In role-playing your side of the debate, try to find some facts or good reasons to support each of the four arguments presented. The appendix will give you some hints on how to proceed in researching this topic.

PRO (Kill the killers.)

1. All actions have consequences; rapists, murderers, kidnappers and the like should realize that there is a price to pay for serious crimes.

2. Punishment, like the death penalty, deters others from committing the same kind of crime. They'll think twice before they kill, rape or kidnap.

3. When a wrong is committed, justice must balance the scales. An eye for an eye, a tooth for a tooth. Society needs to protect itself.

4. It is better for a prisoner to die than to rot in a prison for a lifetime; it's more merciful.

CON (Show mercy.)

1. We should show mercy to the sinner. You can't reform a dead person.

2. There is no proof that capital punishment actually has ever deterred crime. In fact, when there was the first public lynching in England for pickpocketing, the thieves went wild picking the pockets of the spectators.

3. Capital punishment discriminates against the poor who cannot hire fancy lawyers to get them off.

4. The goal of our correctional system is to rehabilitate the criminal, not kill him/her.

For Discussion:

1. After assembling your arguments, debate both sides of the issue.

2. Use the facts and opinions discussed by the class to run a particular case through the STOP sign.

5. An alcoholic friend

You have heard all the arguments against drinking and other drug abuse. But a particular case really bothers you. A friend of yours is rapidly developing into an alcoholic. He cannot seem to do without his liquor. At first, it was a matter of "weekend drinking" alone. Now he seems to need it every day. It is affecting all aspects of his life, even your friendship. Discuss two questions: 1) What can you do for him? 2) What should you do for him?

Discussion:

1. Apply the STOP sign to the problem of teen drinking. Here are some facts:

   - an estimated 10 million Americans drink to excess

   - drinking is blamed for 205,000 deaths a year

   - risk of death from disease, accident or violence is two to six times greater for the problem drinker than for the population at large

   - drinking problems cost society about $43 billion in 1975 in lost production, medical bills and accidents plus other expenses

   - alcohol may be involved in up to one-third of all suicides, half of all murders, half of all traffic deaths and a fourth of all other accidental deaths

   - alcohol is now suspected to be a major factor in child abuse and marital violence

   - in addition to the 10 million adult problem drinkers (7% of all adults), an estimated 3.3 million youths aged 14-17 have drinking problems ranging from trouble in school to car accidents

   - alcohol is the third leading cause of birth defects and is involved in the cause of cancer

   - youthful drinking habits often remain into adulthood

2. Discuss the morality of "smoking-up." Start with an investigation of the latest scientific facts on marijuana.

APPENDIX

Case 3: Helping "Gramps" die

Bibliography: This case involves the topic of euthanasia. The following works can provide some useful background reading should you wish to research the topic in more depth. The bibliography presents the "official" church position on the topic as well as what some modern theologians are saying. The theological opinions represented vary from the "liberal" to the "conservative" sides of the argument.

Church Teaching:

Abbott, S. J., Walter. *The Documents of Vatican II.* New York: America Press, 1966. Read the *Pastoral Constitution on the Church in the Modern World,* No. 27, p. 226.

Hardon, S. J., John. *The Catholic Catechism.* Garden City, New York: Doubleday & Company, Inc., 1975, pp. 329-334. Fr. Hardon gives a good background to the church's teaching.

The Pope Speaks. No. 4 (1958): 395-6. These pages give the classic statement of Pope Pius XII on euthanasia.

Statements of the American Bishops. A packet of statements from both individuals and groups of American bishops on death and dying. Available from NCCB Committee for Pro-Life Activities, 50 cents.

To Live in Christ Jesus. Washington, D.C.: United States Catholic Conference, 1976, pp. 20-22. This is an excellent document by the American bishops on the moral life.

Villot, Cardinal Jean. "The Physician and the Protection of Life," *The Pope Speaks,* Vol. 15, No. 3, 1970. Calls upon Catholic doctors to set standards in medical ethics.

Theological Reflection:

Behnke, John and Sissela Bok, eds. *The Dilemma of Euthanasia.* New York: Doubleday, Anchor Books, 1975. Contains selected articles on euthanasia.

Curran, Charles. *Ongoing Revision: Studies in Moral Theology*. Notre Dame, Indiana: Fides Publications, Inc., 1975, Chapter 5. Fr. Curran is a leading Catholic moral theologian. Chapter 5 is on the topic of the so-called "principle of double effect"—a principle often used in discussing the topic of euthanasia.

Dedek, John F. *Contemporary Medical Ethics*. Mission, Kansas: Sheed Andrews and McMeel, 1975. Chapter 8 is an excellent introductory chapter on euthanasia. It is clear and easy to read.

Dedek, John F. *Titius and Bertha Ride Again: Contemporary Moral Cases*. Mission, Kansas: Sheed Andrews and McMeel. Case 8 gives an excellent introduction to the topic of passive euthanasia.

Hauerwas, Stanley. *Vision & Virtue*. Notre Dame, Indiana: Fides Publishers, Inc., 1974. Chapter 9 gives a topflight discussion on the ethics of death.

Kelly, S. J., Gerald. *Medico-Moral Problems*. St. Louis: The Catholic Hospital Association, 1958. This entire book is the classic text on medical-moral problems referred to often by most theologians.

Kubler-Ross, Elizabeth. *On Death and Dying*. New York: Macmillan, 1969. A classic in the field on death.

————, ed. *Death: The Final Stage of Growth*. Englewood Cliffs, New Jersey: Prentice-Hall, 1975. An excellent series of readings on the spiritual dimensions of death.

Maguire, Daniel. *Death by Choice*. New York: Schocken Books, 1975. This work is considered controversial but the reasoning used by Professor Maguire is excellent.

May, William E. *Human Existence, Medicine and Ethics*. Chicago: Franciscan Herald Press, 1977. Chapter 6 is excellent, but difficult reading. May is a conservative theologian.

McHugh, James T., ed. *Death, Dying and the Law*. Huntington, Indiana: Our Sunday Visitor, Inc., 1976. Excellent background reading.

Shannon, Thomas A., ed. *Bioethics*. New York: Paulist Press, 1976. Part 3 contains some interesting, though difficult, chapters on death and dying.

Weber, Leonard J. *Who Shall Live?* New York: Paulist Press, 1976. Outlines various ethical approaches to dealing with the rights of handicapped persons and the duty of society to protect handicapped persons.

Background Information:

Hippocratic oath: (Taken by doctors)—contains the promise to refuse to give a "deadly drug to any, though it be asked of me."

Directive 28 of the *Ethical and Religious Directives for Catholic Health-Care Facilities:* "Euthanasia (mercy killing) in all its forms is forbidden" (USSC, November, 1971, p. 13).

SUMMARY OF CHURCH TEACHING ON EUTHANASIA

1. *Definitions.* The word "euthanasia" comes from two Greek words meaning a good or happy death. Today, the word has come to mean "an act or method of causing death painlessly, so as to end suffering" (*Webster's New World Dictionary*). In reading about euthanasia, you may run across the following two distinctions:

> a. *Active (or positive or direct) euthanasia:* This refers to the directly willed inducement of death for merciful reasons. This is the term most people mean when they use the word "euthanasia."

> b. *Passive (or negative or indirect) euthanasia:* This refers to allowing oneself or another to die when the person is terminally ill, where there is no obligation to continue life-support systems and where there is no reasonable hope of recovery. You can easily see how there might be confusion over this topic of euthanasia because a person must be very clear on what he or she means. As a result, some moralists think that we should use the word "euthanasia" only for the active intervention to cause death and invent another word like "agathanasia" or "benemortasia" (good death) to define the concept of letting a person die.

2. *Basis of church teaching.* The basis of church teaching is presented in the introductory paragraphs to this chapter. In short, life is a great good given to us by God. Each person has basic dignity derived from being a child of God. Individuals and society must do all that is reasonably necessary to safeguard and preserve human life. No one has an absolute right over his or her life. As persons, we belong to our Father and to one another.

3. *The heart of the teaching.* In essence, Catholic teaching holds that we must take all *ordinary* means to preserve life, even if there is little hope for recovery. However, we are not obligated to use *extraordinary* means to prolong life when there appears to be no hope for the individual. Note, however, that we may use extraordinary means if we wish to do so. This teaching is based on the classic statement on euthanasia by Pope Pius XII. The heart of this teaching resides in what is meant by "ordinary" versus "extraordinary" means. The following gives the common teaching on these two distinctions:

   a. *ordinary means:* "not only normal food, drink and rest but all medicines, treatments and operations which offer a reasonable hope of benefit and which can be obtained and used without excessive pain or other inconvenience";

   b. *extraordinary means:* "all medicines, treatments and operations which cannot be obtained or used without excessive expense, pain or other inconvenience for the patient or others, or which if used would not offer a reasonable hope of benefit to the patient." (These quotes are by Fr. Gerald Ford, S. J., cited by Fr. John Dedek in his *Human Life: Some Moral Issues,* Mission, Kansas: Sheed Andrews and McMeel, 1972, pp. 125-126.)

It should be noted that it is always ordinary and required to use any means necessary to keep the patient free from pain and discomfort, to assist him or her in being lucid and alert (as much as possible). In other words, such procedures are always necessary, even if as a result the person is being indirectly strengthened. Catholic teaching would hold that extraordinary means would be very costly, very unusual, very painful, very difficult, very dangerous, or would achieve very little good in the long run.

In summary, then, the church's teaching says that you may not directly kill someone. Active euthanasia is condemned. (See Vatican II's *Pastoral Constitution on the Church in the Modern World,* No. 27.) However, a person does have the right to make personal decisions affecting how one will encounter his/her own death and dying. Although we must use ordinary means to maintain life, we are not obligated to use extraordinary means. There is a big difference between directly killing a person and failing to use extraordinary means, thus allowing him or her to die a natural death. (You may wish to discuss here the problem in defining exactly what extraordinary means are. What is extraordinary today may very well be ordinary a hundred years from now. A heart transplant comes readily to mind, for example.)

4. *A final word.* The church's teaching tries to protect human life and yet it is a teaching of faith. By saying that one does not have to use extraordinary means to keep a person alive, the church teaches that a person has a right to meet a natural death in peace. Life at any cost can be quite inhuman; for example, living on machines in a comatose state for five years. Our faith is that death is not the end of human existence; rather, it is a transition to a new, glorious life with the risen Lord. Furthermore, Christianity has consistently taught that good can come from suffering, especially when it is joined to the suffering of our Savior. This is not to say that Christians do not recognize suffering as evil; it means that in the light of Jesus' death and resurrection it can be given meaning.

Case 4: Kill the killers?

Bibliography: The best way to get into a topic like this (and many others) is to consult recent articles written on the topic. The *Reader's Guide to Periodical Literature* will be of great help in directing you to secular magazines. You should also be familiar with the *Catholic Periodical and Literature Index.* This resource can direct you to excellent articles in magazines such as *U.S. Catholic, St. Anthony Messenger, America, Commonweal,* the *National Catholic Reporter* and others. There have been some excellent articles about capital punishment printed in these periodicals in recent years.

For starters, you may wish to consult the *New Catholic Encyclopedia* under the heading "Capital Punishment." Also, these books will help:

Barclay, William. *The Ten Commandments for Today.* Grand Rapids, Michigan: Wm. Eerdmans Publishing Co., 1973, pp. 67-79. Barclay, a Protestant, presents good historical background and all the arguments pro and con from the viewpoint of a scripture scholar.

Baum, Robert and James Randell. *Ethical Arguments for Analysis.* New York: Holt, Rinehart and Winston, Inc., 1973, Chapter 10. This book presents a number of readings—good short articles—on both sides of the issue.

Grisez, Germain and Russell Shaw. *Beyond the New Morality: The Responsibilities of Freedom.* Notre Dame: University of Notre Dame Press, 1974, Chapter 14. This is an excellent book on Christian ethics.

Lawler, O.F.M., Cap., Ronald, Donald W. Wuerl and Thomas Comerford Lawler. *The Teaching of Christ.* Huntington, Indiana: Our Sunday Visitor Press, 1976, pp. 317-318. This Catholic catechism presents the church's position. (You may wish to consult other catechisms as well.)

Stevens, Edward. *Making Moral Decisions.* New York: Paulist Press, 1969, pp. 76-81. Stevens lines up the pro and con arguments very well in these pages.

BRIEF SUMMARY OF CHURCH TEACHING ON CAPITAL PUNISHMENT

1. Traditionally, Catholic theologians have accepted the right of the state to use capital punishment in cases of serious crimes.

2. However, more recently, some Catholic theologians and bishops have questioned the morality of capital punishment. In light of a Christian's profound respect for all human life, they question whether capital punishment truly deters crime and they question its apparent vindictiveness (revengefulness). In their recent pastoral letter *To Live in Christ Jesus,* the bishops remind us to focus on the conditions that cause crime and to take a hard look at our penal system which is often unjust and a source of increase in crime.

For further discussion and analysis:

You may wish to discuss and research the following topics in the area of life issues:

1. Cloning
2. Genetic manipulation
3. Environmental pollution
4. Organ transplants
5. War
6. Artificial insemination
7. Test-tube babies
8. Use of drugs
9. Use of alcohol
10. Homosexuality

9

Solving Moral Problems: Truth and Justice

What we have in us of the image of God is the love of truth and justice.
—Demosthenes

This chapter, like the preceding one, will continue the discussion of moral problems. Presented here are cases related to the themes of truth and justice. The cases are preceded by a few exercises, a brief discussion on truth and justice and some relevant quotations from church documents on the theme of social justice. An appendix at the end of the chapter includes ideas for more research and involvement on the justice issue and a bibliography which should prove helpful in research on the topics under consideration.

Let us begin this chapter by looking at a few truth and justice issues. Below are two lists of potential moral problems. Rank-order each list from (1) the most severe violation of truth and justice to (5) the least severe violation of truth and justice. Compare your rankings with those of your classmates and then discuss the questions at the end of the exercise.

TRUTH AND JUSTICE ISSUES:

LIST A

—— A teenager is involved in an accident with a parked car late at night on a dark street. It is a dangerous neighborhood. Only slight damage is done. He leaves the scene of the accident, failing to give any word of damage done.

—— A disgruntled student steals her chemistry teacher's grade book at the end of the term. The teacher has no other record of student progress.

—— For a small fee, a 21-year-old college student purchases alcohol for younger students under age.

—— A very generous family man gives a substantial portion of his paycheck each week to the poor, thus denying his family members luxuries and sometimes even necessities.

—— A school system has a subtle policy of funneling 90 percent of the athletic budget to boys' sports, thus neglecting to build up the girls' program.

LIST B

—— You walk away from a fight where a classmate has been unfairly jumped.

—— You are a dining room attendant at a restaurant and have a habit of lifting for yourself some of the tips meant for the waiters.

—— You are asked to write a letter of recommendation for a fellow worker who is rather mediocre on the job. You write a very flattering letter.

———— In a discussion on salaries for different professions, you argue very loudly and strongly in order to justify the high wages of sports figures versus the relatively low salaries of teachers.

———— You have devised a way to bilk a vending machine of its change. You tell no one of your system.

Discussion:

1. In your estimation, are there any cases listed above which are perfectly all right? Explain.

2. Why did you choose as you did? Was it the number of people involved? the harm done?

HONESTY

Honesty includes the virtues of truthfulness and justice. Very few issues command our attention today to the degree that honesty does. Truthfulness is especially a much-discussed topic. Crimes against truth abound everywhere. They range from a clerk short-changing a customer to false advertising, graft in politics, cheating on exams and on income tax forms, laziness on the job and all kinds of white-collar crime, perhaps the most often committed crime in our country. The 1970's saw the era of Watergate and governmental spying on citizens. The tragedy of these events is that the people involved thought that getting caught was what they did wrong.

When a person says, "Take my word for it" or "You have my word of honor," you know that person wants to be believed. Yet, aren't these expressions cheap today? Don't they give rise to the so-called "credibility gap" which we find between the generations and between government and its citizens? Perhaps more than anyone else, young people cannot tolerate a hypocrite. What is hypocrisy other than a person not being true to himself or herself and to others? Truth and honesty are the touchstones of a person's character. They engender trust and harmonious relationships. Their absence brings suspicion, deceit and mistrust.

Jesus was very concerned to show that the truth will set us free. And what is truth? Truth usually corresponds to two realities. The first is that my words correspond to my thoughts and to reality. Lying is the opposite of truth in this category. The second is that my deeds correspond to my words. Stealing and other forms of hyprocritical deception are the very antithesis of truth in this category. We tend to admire the person who is truthful and straight-forward in both his or her words and actions. These qualities are the sign of a "together" person, an honorable individual, one who says what is meant and does what is said.

The other side of the honesty coin is justice, that is, giving to others what is their due. Take the following justice survey. Put an X next to the statements with which you agree and an O next to the items with which you disagree.

JUSTICE SURVEY

———   1. No one should be refused membership in a club on the basis of sex.

———   2. As a homeowner you have the right to sell or not to sell to anyone you please.

———   3. Medical and law schools should establish quota systems to admit minority groups (perhaps not as academically qualified as others) in order to redress the wrongs committed against these groups in the past.

———   4. Poor people have no right to goods or services for which they cannot pay.

———   5. The state should provide free abortions to anyone on request because all women have the right to control their own bodies.

———   6. America's disproportionate consumption of the world's goods while so many are in abject poverty is objectively immoral.

―――― 7. Every American has the right to a college education.

―――― 8. Minimum job standards must be established for certain professions. For example, it is OK for police forces to weed out overweight patrolmen.

―――― 9. Health care should be provided by the state to all whether they can pay or not.

―――― 10. Private schools have the right to exclude individuals who cannot meet their admission standards.

Discussion:

a. What is justice?

b. Are there any statements which you would like to qualify before either agreeing or disagreeing with them?

c. Is justice something that has to be earned? Or is it something a person deserves because of his or her dignity as a person?

JUSTICE

Justice is the minimum love we owe persons because of who they are as God's creatures with basic human dignity. It is the least we can do to respond to others. Justice naturally flows from a respect for life. It is a reaction to others in view of what they are. There are three kinds of justice: commutative, distributive and legal.

Commutative justice. This form of justice deals with fairness of exchange. It is that due in relationships between individuals or between social entities such as nations or corporations. For example, if I sell you my used car for $500 with the promise that it runs, in justice it had better run. Another example would be treaties between nations.

Distributive justice. This kind of justice refers to fairness in sharing the goods of the world. More specifically, it deals with a fair distribution of goods and burdens to the citizens by the state representatives. Sharing the wealth of the land, including natural resources and food, with the poor and disadvantaged is an example of distributive justice. Fostering the common good by allowing the development of individuals and small groups within a nation would also exemplify this type of justice. What militates against distributive justice is gross discrimination which favors special interest groups, thus resulting in exploitation of the weak and helpless. A mentality that a person has to merit (earn) the basic necessities and rights due everyone by his or her very human dignity is also contrary to distributive justice.

Legal justice. This form of justice governs the debts an individual owes to the social group in order to help build up the common good. For example, the payment of taxes, obeying laws, voting, involvement in social action programs and the rendering of military service are all forms of legal justice obligations.

Commutative justice governs relationships among individuals; distributive justice deals with relationships of the larger social group to the individual; and legal justice refers to relationships of the individual to the larger social group. There needs to be a delicate balance between all three forms of justice. Unfortunately, in our American society, we have tended to be overly concerned about commutative and legal justice to the detriment of distributive justice. For example, most of our court cases deal with suits between individuals or in regard to corporate relationships. This manifests a good emphasis on protecting individual liberty. Our society is also quite interested in stressing the obligations the individual has in regard to the state. Again, this is a good thing and should not be forgotten. However, what has suffered is a fair distribution of the world's goods to the poor and the powerless. There is something wrong in this rich country of ours when there is still such widespread poverty. In addition, there is something grossly unfair about eight percent of the world's population consuming 35 to 40 percent of the world's goods. Yet, it should be pointed out that

America does spend millions of dollars' worth of energy per year in order to produce food for the Third World. On the international level, it is true that the rich get richer and the poor get poorer. This can only happen when distributive justice is forgotten.

As Catholics, we can be very proud of the teaching of our popes on the topic of social justice (or distributive justice) over the past several decades. They have spoken very loudly and clearly on the obligation all men and women have to see that God's created goods are better distributed to all his creatures. We will take a look at some of this social justice teaching in the next section of the chapter.

Two asides:

No. 1: You may have read about a famous medical case which took place in recent years. A 39-year-old man was dying of a rare form of a bone marrow disease. He requested his cousin, the only suitable donor they could find, to undergo a painful operation, the purpose of which would be a bone marrow transplant. The cousin refused, saying he himself was in poor health and that his sick cousin had only a 50-50 chance to survive even with the transplant. In effect, he was saying he was under no obligation (commutative justice) to donate his bone marrow. His sick cousin went to court to force the donation. The judge in the case declared that the cousin did not have to submit to the operation since he was under no legal obligation to do so. The sick cousin died several weeks later (forgiving his reluctant cousin) of some other complication of his disease. The question is: In light of distributive justice, did the cousin have the duty to donate some of his bone marrow?

No. 2: Some people talk about a fourth kind of justice called retributive justice. This refers to punishment due crime or wrongdoing. With your classmates, discuss the following retributive justice case: On a special free day, three seniors at a Catholic school were caught in a prank at a neighborhood girls' school. They ran through the cafeteria with masks over their heads throwing water balloons at the girls. The school authorities notified their principal. Their school had obviously been given a bad name; the principal was quite upset over the incident. He wants to throw the three malefactors out of the school in order to prevent any similar kind of incident in the future. Your group is to visit the principal and advise him on the "just" thing to do. Give reasons for your advice.

THE CHURCH AND JUSTICE

The pope and bishops have spoken often about the Christian's obligation to respond to the neighbor in need. As members of Christ's body entrusted with the mandate to teach, our leaders have been very concerned about the "least of these" referred to by Jesus in Matthew's Gospel. Their teaching is an attempt to put into action the warning sounded by St. John: "I ask you, how can God's love survive in a man who has enough of this world's goods yet closes his heart to his brother when he sees him in need?" (1 Jn 3:17).

As the list of documents in the appendix to this chapter will attest, the church's social teaching is quite exhaustive. Below are just a few sample quotes from these documents which show the basis for the church's concern for social justice. The words pretty much speak for themselves. This section concludes with six summary points on what Christians can do to foster social justice. These points are summarized from the Canadian Conference of Catholic Bishops' Labor Day Message of 1976.

> Since all men possess a rational soul and are created in God's likeness, since they have the same nature and origin, have been redeemed by Christ, and enjoy the same divine calling and destiny, the basic equality of all must receive increasingly greater recognition. . . . Moreover, although rightful differences exist between men, the equal dignity of persons demands that a more humane and just condition of life be brought about. For excessive economic and social differences between members of the one human family or population groups cause scandal, and militate against social justice, equity, the dignity of the human person, as well as social and international peace (*Pastoral Constitution on the Church in the Modern World*, 29).

> God intended the earth and all that it contains for the use of every human being and people. Thus, as all men follow justice and unite in charity, created goods should abound for them on a reason-

able basis. . . . For the rest, the right to have a share of earthly goods sufficient for oneself and one's family belongs to everyone. The Fathers and Doctors of the Church held this view, teaching that men are obliged to come to the relief of the poor, and to do so not merely out of their superfluous goods. If a person is in extreme necessity, he has the right to take from others what he himself needs (*Pastoral Constitution on the Church in the Modern World,* 69).

Love implies an absolute demand for justice, namely a recognition of the dignity and rights of one's neighbor (*Justice in the World,* Synod of Bishops).

It is agreed that in our time, the common good is chiefly guaranteed when personal rights and duties are maintained (*Pacem in Terris,* Pope John XXIII).

No one is justified in keeping for his exclusive use what he does not need, when others lack necessities (*Populorum Progressio,* 23).

The members of mankind share the same basic rights and duties, as well as the same supernatural destiny. Within a country which belongs to each one, all should be equal before the law, find equal admittance to economic, cultural, civic and social life—and benefit from a fair sharing of the nation's riches (*Call to Action,* Apostolic Letter of Pope Paul VI).

WHAT CHRISTIANS CAN DO

• *Understand the true meaning of the gospel message of justice.* This calls for various Christian groups to study and act on specific injustices in light of the gospel.

• *Modify our more affluent life-styles.* Toning down our extravagant way of living will not by itself overcome the gross disparities among people. But it can renew our spirit and open our hearts to the plight of the poor in our midst.

• *Listen to the victims of injustice in our own communities.* By listening to the oppressed we can learn much more about the attitudes and structures that cause human suffering and what can be done about them.

• *Speak out against injustice in our communities.* As citizens, we have the duty to exercise our freedom and responsibility to speak out on specific issues. Unless our voices unite, those in power will not heed the cries of injustice.

• *Participate in causes which help to overcome injustice.* The goal is social justice. The means to this goal is political action.

• *Provide help to poor and oppressed groups.* As followers of Jesus, we have the responsibility not only to feed the hungry but to increase their power to change the causes of hunger.

SOME CASES FOR DISCUSSION

1. An enterprising student

You may have read about an especially enterprising 22-year-old student who loved to do research in libraries. He pored over declassified information in the Library of Congress and wrote a 400-page document on how to build a number of different kinds of atomic bombs. He had no particularly strong background in physics. He wanted to get the research report published in book form for the sake of making some money. When the government found out about the young man's research (he told them), it confiscated the report, classified the information and forbade the student from discussing the paper with anyone who lacks a special "Q" nuclear security clearance. In exchange for the confiscated report, the student requested that the government hire him as a consultant. The government refused to do so, claiming that he had no special skill that could be used. The student is without his paper, under a ban which prevents him from discussing it lest he be criminally prosecuted, and without a job.

Discuss:

1. Is what the government has done to the student just? Was the student's research using only declassified government documents moral? Explain in light of the STOP sign.

2. If you were the student in question, what would you do now?

3. Has the freedom of the press been abridged in this case? The freedom of speech? Why or why not?

---

2. To be a judge

In 1978, the Supreme Court justices ruled on one of the most controversial cases in American legal history in the famous Bakke case. If you recall, the issue was whether schools could accept academically less qualified students from minority groups in order to help redress some of the decades of discrimination against those same groups. The problem with accepting less qualified students was that there was a type of "reverse discrimination" against other students since there were not enough places in the entering class. In other words, there are many more qualified applicants for law and medical schools than there are positions in the class. The up-shot of the case was a delicately nuanced decision which allowed Alan Bakke to go to school but at the same time one that gave schools the go-ahead to try and find positions in entering classes for minority groups, without constructing quota systems.

Discuss:

1. Do a little research on this case. Divide the class into two groups. In a debate, one group should present the arguments for the California university which failed to admit Mr. Bakke. The other group should argue for Mr. Bakke. Try to reconstruct the arguments which came before the Supreme Court.

2. As a group, decide if justice was done in the case. Comment on which kind of justice is being talked about.

3. In light of the STOP sign and church teaching on social justice, comment on the morality of this case or similar types of cases. Put special emphasis on the T of the STOP sign, namely, alternatives and con-sequences.

---

3. Politics and money

It is the month of May and you badly need money to go to a prom. A very close friend invited you to the prom and you would very much like to go. At the present time you do not have a job or any outside source of income to raise the necessary funds for the dance and the fun weekend to follow.

However, another friend tells you that it is possible to pick up $150 by working for a prominent local politician in his primary campaign. The only problem is that he is a strong advocate for abortion on demand—an issue which you are strongly against.

Would you work on the primary campaign?

Discuss:

1. Explain your decision.

2. Do you think you would compromise your values if you worked on the campaign?

3. What are the issues in the situation?

4. If you would work on the campaign, how could you justify it to your friends, many of whom know about your strong feelings on the abortion issue?

4. A man for all seasons

One of the most famous English saints is Thomas More. His life story is beautifully and sensitively told in a play entitled *A Man for All Seasons* by Robert Bolt. More was the chancellor of England, the most powerful man next to the king, Henry VIII. Henry VIII was a Catholic who divorced his wife against church law. In trying to justify his decision, the king ran into conflict with the pope. Thus, he decided to make himself the head of the church in England. More refused to either condone Henry's divorce or take a required oath of allegiance to Henry as head of the church.

More's family and friends begged him to take Henry's oath of allegiance. More refused, was given a lengthy prison term and was finally beheaded after a famous trial where lies and false accusations were made against him. He died putting loyalty to his God and church above loyalty to the king.

Discuss:

1. Was More just to his family?

2. Does our era produce men and women like Thomas More? Do people today believe that there are causes worth dying for?

3. Are there any causes which you would not compromise? Is there anything or anyone you would die for? Would you do what Thomas More did?

4. You might wish to read Bolt's play. If so, discuss More's decision in light of the STOP sign.

5. Pope Paul VI and Social Justice

The late Pope Paul VI was noted for his visionary teachings on social justice and his work for world peace. In 1967, he wrote a very important encyclical entitled *Populorum Progressio (On the Development of Peoples).* In that encyclical he was very concerned about what he described as the sick state of the world where there is such an imbalance in the sharing of the world's goods. He made four strong recommendations in that encyclical which would help poor nations develop. They are:

1. *Individual charity (Populorum Progressio,* 44-45): The Christian has the obligation to give to the "least of these." Gifts to the missions, Care, Bishops' Relief Funds, private charity are all examples which should be increased to help the poor people of the world.

2. *The creation of a world fund* (51): This international bank would be created by a kind of tax on the rich nations of the world through cutbacks on military expenditures. Poor nations could borrow this money in their efforts to develop more advanced industrialized economies.

3. *Rectify trade relationships* (57-61): Pope Paul called for more justice in the way the major powers trade with poor countries. He asked that the same standards of justice which have been developed within a rich country to protect the poor and disadvantaged be applied outside a nation's borders so that the poor nations have a chance to compete equally on the world's trade market.

4. *Create and support an international organization which will coordinate and support a new judicial order* (78): Here, the pope called for an international organization like the United Nations with real political and judicial clout to help prevent the rich from exploiting the poor and to aid the poor in their development.

Discuss:

1. Are these recommendations realistic? What are the alternatives?

2. What prevents rich nations from helping the poor to a greater degree?

3. What are some possible consequences of not helping to a greater degree? (Here you might consult the encyclical. It lists some of the consequences.)

4. What is nationalism? How might it prevent countries from coming to the aid of the poor? Is supernationalism moral? Explain.

APPENDIX

Bibliography: There are literally thousands of books published on the topic of justice. Many of them published in recent years are outstanding. Below is listed a very small sample of some of the best. You may wish to consult some of them in doing your research on this theme.

Church documents: Here are the major documents on social justice in the last two decades. You can find these published in many different forms.

Mater et Magistra (1961)—Pope John XXIII's encyclical letter which treats primarily the rights and duties of countries in the area of economic development. Its English title is *Mother and Teacher.*

Pacem in Terris (1963)—Pope John XXIII's encyclical letter. Excellent on the topic of how rich nations ought to treat poor nations. Its English title is *Peace on Earth.*

Pastoral Constitution on the Church in the Modern World (1965) —An outstanding document from the Second Vatican Council. Discusses the church's mission to the contemporary world.

Populorum Progressio (1967)—Pope Paul VI's revolutionary encyclical letter. English title is *On the Development of
Peoples.*

A Call to Action (1971)—A key work by Pope Paul VI on the
theme of international justice.

Justice in the World (1971)—Composed by the world synod of
bishops.

Liberty and Justice for All (1975)—A work composed by the
American bishops. Especially illuminating in light of the
American bicentennial.

To Live in Christ Jesus (1976)—Another important work by the
American bishops on moral issues such as the family and
national/international justice.

O'Brien, David J. and Thomas J. Shannon, eds. *Renewing the
Earth—Catholic Documents on Peace, Justice and Liber-
ation.* Garden City, New York: Image Books, 1977. Besides presenting some of the key documents listed above,
this collection contains an excellent short overview of Catholic social teaching through the ages.

Other Works:

Burghardt, S. J., Walter J. *Seven Hungers.* Washington, D.C.:
United States Catholic Conference (USCC), 1976. An
excellent theological work on the basic human needs.

Byron, S. J., William. *Toward Stewardship: An Interim Ethic of
Poverty, Pollution and Power.* New York: Paulist Press,
1975. The last chapter questions whether Christ really con-
signed the poor to be with us always.

de Broucker, Jose. *Dom Helder Camara: The Violence of a Peace-
maker.* Maryknoll, New York: Orbis Books. A readable
biography of one of the great churchmen working for peace
in the Third World.

de Jesus, Carolina Maria. *Child of the Dark.* New York: Signet,
1962. A moving autobiography by a courageous woman
who lived in abject poverty in a Brazilian favela.

Dunne, George H. *The Right to Development.* New York: Paulist
Press, 1974. A stimulating and readable little book giving
a moral argument in support of the Third World's right to
development.

Kerans, Patrick. *Sinful Social Structures*. New York: Paulist Press, 1974. Argues that sin infects not just individuals but the very structures of society.

The Radical Bible. Maryknoll, New York: Orbis Books, 1972. Very effective in showing the applicability of biblical teaching to the world situation.

Ryan, William. *Blaming the Victim*. Vintage Press, 1972. Shows how we blame the victims of poverty rather than the real villain, the inequality in American society.

Simon, Arthur. *Bread for the World*. New York: Paulist Press, 1975. A compelling source of information on the hunger problem with lots of concrete suggestions on what one can do to help.

Sourcebook on Poverty, Development and Justice. Campaign for Human Development, USCC. A collection of essays exploring various aspects of the question, "What does it mean in the United States to be a Christian, carrying out the social mission of the church?"

Wilkins, Ronald J. *Achieving Social Justice*. Dubuque, Iowa: Wm. C. Brown Publishing Co., 1976. A popular high school text on social justice. A good resource.

Activities: One of the best ways to learn about the morality of social justice is firsthand experience as well as more in-depth research. Some of these might be helpful.

1. *Scripture assignment.* Check out the following references and make a short report on biblical teaching on justice.

> Lv 19:9-10 (portion of harvest for the poor)
> Dt 10:14-19 (the Lord and justice)
> Ps 146:5-8 (the just Lord who feeds the hungry)
> Prv 21:13 (hear the cries of the poor)
> Am 5:21-24 (justice)
> Mt 14:15-21 (Jesus feeding the multitude)
> Lk 4:16-21 (helping the poor and oppressed)
> Lk 12:32-48 (to whom much is given is much required)
> Lk 16:19-31 (rich man and Lazarus)
> Jn 6:1-14 (Jesus as the bread for the world)

Acts 2:42-47 (early Christians sharing)
1 Cor 11:17-33 (selfishness in the Christian community)
1 Tm 6:6-19 (be rich in generosity)
Jas 2:14-17; 26 (faith without works is dead)

2. *Minireports.* Give a 10-minute report on one of the following:

tax system
public housing
the American Indian
wage and price controls
aid to nonpublic schools
corporations and social justice
labor unions and power
urban progress
welfare programs
multinational corporations
international government
propaganda and mass media
censorship
revolutions
gay rights
women's rights

3. Locate local civic and religious organizations that need your help. Report on their needs. Participate in a fund-raising activity to arouse public attention to the problem at hand.

4. *Projects.* As an individual or a class, participate in one of the following:

Collect clothing for the needy
Take some poor kids to an amusement park
Visit shut-ins
Cut lawns or shovel snow for old people
Visit a nursing home
Check out food prices in a suburban versus an inner-city
  grocery store

Tutor some elementary school kids
Teach retarded kids how to swim
Invite a guest missionary into class to speak

SUMMARY

1. The touchstone of a person's character is honesty. Honesty includes both truth and justice.

2. Truth-telling involves not only speech but also being true to one's verbal commitments, following through on what one says.

3. Commutative justice involves fairness of exchange; distributive justice concerns sharing the goods of the earth; legal justice deals with the debts an individual owes his or her community.

4. The term "retributive justice" concerns punishment due wrongdoing.

5. The church has spoken often and clearly on the theme of social justice. This teaching flows from Jesus' mandate to respond to the poor, the oppressed and the powerless.

6. One of the best ways to learn about social justice is through firsthand research.

10

Reasoning Morally and Conclusion

I would rather be right than president.
—Henry Clay

The best portion of a good man's life is his little, name-less, unremembered acts of kindness.
—William Wordsworth

This final chapter covers three topics. First, we will take a look at the typical ways people arrive at moral conclusions and then say a word about moral heroism. Next, several more cases will be presented for your discussion and analysis. Finally, a brief self-check quiz will be given on the themes of the book. The purpose of the quiz will be to review the book and help you identify areas which might need more clarification.

MORAL REASONING

Imagine for a minute that you are involved in the following experiment on a college campus. A famous psychology professor offers to pay you some money to participate in a learning experiment. He takes you to his lab. In the lab is a partition separating two areas. In the first area is a learning box which is connected to some electrodes and a shock box. The strength of the voltage going through the electrodes is controlled by the teaching station on the other side of the partition. The professor administers a very small shock to you to indicate that the learning station is in working order.

The purpose of the experiment is to find out the effectiveness of electrical shocks on how well a person remembers. Your task is to assume a position at the teaching station, read off lists of nonsense words to a learner and, if necessary, administer successively more powerful shocks of voltage to a learner who will be strapped in a chair, connected to electrodes at the learning station. What would you do?

This experiment was actually conducted by Dr. Stanley Milgram. What he was testing was not the learning rate of students connected to the electrodes but how far his paid helpers would go in administering electric shocks to the student. In reality, the person who played the part of the learner was a "dupe" who was instructed to pretend he was shocked by yelling and then eventually passing out as the voltage increased. The person administering the shocks could not see the dupe on the other side of the partition. To use a poor pun, the results of Milgram's research were revolting. A full two-thirds of the people who participated in it went all the way and administered the full 300 volts to the person they thought was incorrectly answering the questions! They did this even after the dupe screamed in excruciating agony and eventually after he "blacked out."

Almost to a person, those who went all the way said they followed through on the experiment because the person in authority asked them to do so. They assumed the researcher knew what he was doing and, after all, who were they to question? This experiment took place in America in this decade. Certainly, it must remind us of those Nazis who after World War II said they were only following orders when they committed war crimes.

Milgram's research is frightening. It argues rather convincingly that the majority of people tend to conform under any and all circumstances. Conformity is often the tyrant which keeps us from doing the right thing. Why do people conform? There are many reasons why people tend to go along with the crowd. First, they do it in order to be accepted and to avoid disapproval. One of the basic human needs is to be accepted, and so we naturally try to do things that will win others' approval. Second, by conforming we tend to see ourselves as correct. "After all, if everyone else is doing it, it must be OK" is the reasoning here. A third reason for conformity is to avoid holding an idea contrary to the group. Conformists often flow with the crowd and feel uncomfortable with original ideas. Two more reasons for conformity can be good reasons: We conform to keep the group together and to achieve goals that are best attained through the group. Of course, these could be bad reasons, too, depending on the reasons for the group cohesion and the goals. But there are many times when these last two reasons for conformity are absolutely necessary in order to survive.

It is the first three reasons, however, that can make for what is known as the tyranny of the majority. Doing the right thing often calls for going against the majority, standing alone, being a hero. We shall return to this theme shortly, but let us first look at the research of Dr. Lawrence Kohlberg of Harvard University who has spent his life studying the way people do moral reasoning. Kohlberg is also a psychologist. His interest is in how people develop and he has concluded that people tend to reason in one of six stages at one of three levels. These are briefly described below.

Level 1: Preconventional

Stage 1: Avoid Punishment. A person at this stage judges the goodness or badness of an act by its physical consequences. A person does the right thing to avoid punishment; he or she may do the wrong thing only if there is no chance of getting caught. Such a person is governed both by the fear of the power of authority and by a submission to that superior power. Someone who would reason at this stage might say that the captain in the lifeboat case should not do what he did for fear of being convicted and punished. Note that the judgment on the rightness or wrongness of what the captain did is in terms of avoiding punishment.

Stage 2: Personal Usefulness. This stage of moral thinking is represented by the slogan: "I'll scratch your back if you'll scratch mine." What is right is what satisfies one's own needs and occasionally the needs of others. For example, a person reasoning at this stage may decide to go out of his or her way to do a good deed for someone else, but only if there might be some reward in it.

Level 2: Conventional

The preconventional level of moral reasoning is usually the level of thinking of children. The conventional level, on the other hand, represents the moral thinking of the vast majority of people in our society.

Stage 3: Good Boy/Nice Girl. A person at this stage reasons out moral issues in a way to please and help others in order to get approval or avoid disapproval. At this stage, one maintains, supports and justifies the order within the group. Moral thinking is marked by conformity to the standard ideas of what is the will of the group to which one wants to gain acceptance. Remember the Tom and Jack drug case from Chapter 2? If Tom thought that telling on Jack would result in his being ridiculed by his friends, Tom would probably not reveal Jack's drug dealing.

Stage 4: Law and Order. Kohlberg maintains that of all the six stages, most American adults are at stage 4 which holds the value of obedience to rules for their own sake as necessary to maintain order. Right behavior here consists of doing one's duty. What is right is what maintains the order of the larger social group. Moral thinking at this stage would hold that any flaws in the system are due to the failure of individuals to obey the system. If Tom were at this stage in his conscience struggle to turn Jack in to the authorities, he might well do it in order to uphold the law. If so, Tom might be reasoning that loyalty to one's friends sometimes has to give way to loyalty to the larger social group and the laws which help maintain that group.

Level 3: Postconventional

Because of his studies, Kohlberg has concluded that only a minority of people go beyond convention (custom) in their moral reasoning. Furthermore, he claims that very few people ever consistently reason at stage 6 on moral issues.

Stage 5: Social Contract. In a way, this stage is a further development over stage 4, just as all the stages are more sophisticated than the ones that precede them. Here, a person reasons for the principles behind the laws. The fact that people can both make and change laws is recognized here. One may work to change the law for the sake of society, especially if the change will make the community more self-respecting. Law is not seen as something permanently fixed but something that can change as situations and people change. The framers of the American Constitution reasoned at stage 5.

Stage 6: Personal Conscience. The most advanced stage of moral reasoning is stage 6, where the right is a decision of personal conscience in accord with ethical principles that apply to all persons everywhere. These principles include justice, the equality and reciprocity of human rights, and the respect for the dignity of human beings as individual persons. If in the lifeboat case the captain had not judged on the basis of the "survival of the fittest," but on who and what the occupants of the lifeboat were as fellow human beings, he may have reasoned at this stage. A stage 6 moral thinker refuses to judge the value of a person on what he or she can do but on who the individual is as a fellow human being with rights.

Kohlberg's research helps to see how different people reason about moral issues; it helps to see "where people are coming from" in a debate over moral issues. He maintains that people have to pass through various stages as they progress up the ladder of moral reasoning. Furthermore, he claims that very few people reach the highest level. This, of course, should not make us stereotype or put people into boxes. We learn from one another. Even being able to reason at a very sophisticated level does not mean that a person will do the right thing. Conversely, a person can do the right thing regardless of how he or she reasons morally. You may refrain from murder because you know that you are not being just if you do murder (stage 6); I may refrain from murder because I fear that I may be caught (stage 1). You may have a better reason but at least we have both done the right thing.

When it comes to making moral decisions, the Christian— the follower of Jesus—is called not only to see things as clearly as he or she can in light of the Christian vision but also to act heroically. Christian morality calls for us to be our own persons, to assume responsibility, to suffer for our beliefs. We look to heroes like St. Francis of Assisi who gave unselfishly to the poor because he knew that they were his brothers and sisters in Christ. We look to modern-day heroes like Dorothy Day who witnesses against the insanity of war because she finds it quite difficult to reconcile mass killing with the call of Jesus. We look to Pope John XXIII whose humility and vision gave him the courage to stand out and lead the church into a period of dialogue with the modern world. To be a moral person means to be a person who stands out like the Nazi soldier in World War II who refused to shoot innocent citizens on command and, as a result, was lined up against the wall and shot with the victims.

In the final analysis, to be moral means to look to our greatest hero, Jesus Christ, who was willing to die for us. His mission of kindness and love met with all kinds of opposition, but he refused to back away from it. He stood up and was counted as the most dependable of all humans. His example and his life in us give us the strength (if we but use it) to love the unlovable, to resist the temptations to go along with the crowd, to be his disciples who stand out from others in doing the right thing.

For Discussion:

At what stage was Jesus teaching in the following scripture passages? Can you explain any apparent discrepancies?

- Mt 25: 31-42 (the Last Judgment)
- Lk 20: 20-26 (the coin of tribute)
- Mt 18: 21-22 (how often to forgive)

CONFORMITY IQ

On the following continuums measuring whether you would be likely to stand alone or to follow the lead of the majority, mark an X where you would tend to be.

a. Cheat on an exam when everyone else is doing it.

stand	conform
alone	

b. Pick up litter in a school hallway when no one else is.

stand	conform
alone	

c. Take drugs at a party when everyone else is.

stand	conform
alone	

d. Defend someone who is being mocked out when everyone is laughing at him.

stand	conform
alone	

e. Vote for more taxes for welfare recipients in an election where very few people support the levy.

stand	conform
alone	

f. Stop to help a broken-down car on a freeway late at night.

stand	conform
alone	

g. Go to daily Mass when none of your friends do.

stand	conform
alone	

Discuss:

1. In each of the situations above, what are the risks involved in not conforming?

2. Share your answers and reasons for choosing with your classmates.

SOME FINAL CASES

This section of the last chapter will present a few more cases to enable you to apply what you learned in this book. Good luck with them.

Miracle Cure

Reginald works for a prestigious university. He has recently discovered a cure for a rare, but deadly, blood disease. He is trying to decide if he should make his results known immediately or publish them in a national journal. If he waits for publication in the journal (six months away) he will almost surely be given lots of attention and win some important consulting jobs that will pay him handsomely. He would use the money to pay for the education of his retarded child. But if he waits, at least five people will die of the blood disease in this country alone.

Discuss:

1. If you were Reginald what would you do? What are your reasons?

2. Would it be immoral not to reveal the research findings right away? (Consult the STOP sign.)

3. In Kohlberg's terms, at what stage was your answer in question 1?

Centerfold

Sue is a very attractive model. She has always refused to pose in the nude, but recently she was offered $10,000 to pose for a centerfold in a "soft-core" porn magazine. Normally, she would not give the offer a second thought. However, she has just seen a national television program on world hunger and was deeply moved by it. She vowed then that she would try to raise some money for the starving children she saw in the program. She is tempted to take the lucrative job offer and give the money to the poor.

Discuss:

1. If Sue were your sister, what would you advise her? Why?

2. In Kohlberg's terms, at what stage is your answer?

Bum

You are walking downtown one day alone on a cold winter day. A gentle, but obviously derelict older man comes up to you and asks you for 25 cents for coffee. You have the money. The first thought that comes to mind is the parable of the Good Samaritan. The second thought that comes to mind is that the derelict will probably spend the money for some wine.

Discuss:

1. What would you do and why?

2. Could the STOP sign help you in this situation? Explain.

Good Luck

Gerald embezzled $500 from his employer. He took the money to the racetrack and put it on a horse which had a 10-1 chance to win. Unbelievably, his horse won. He is now having regrets about stealing from his employer so he is contemplating returning the money. But he feels entitled to keep his winnings. If he returns the money, may he keep what he won? Explain your answer.

Job Offer

For about a month you have been doing volunteer work for some underprivileged kids. You really enjoy it and consider it one of the most fulfilling things you have ever done. But you have been offered a job at a local fast-food outlet. You don't need the money for any necessities, but the job would enable you to buy the car you have always wanted. What would you do and why? Would it be wrong for you to take the job? Explain.

Quiz on Book

The following little quiz tests your knowledge of what you have studied in the book. The answers appear at the end of the quiz with appropriate page numbers in case you want to review. Thanks for reading this far and good luck.

1. ———— The kind of justice which is concerned about the fairness of sharing the world's goods is known as:

   a. commutative
   b. legal
   c. retributive
   d. distributive
   e. all of these

2. ———— Which of the following would ordinarily constitute "venial sinfulness"?

   a. adultery
   b. sarcasm
   c. blasphemy
   d. murder
   e. none of these

3. ———— The Supreme Court decision (1973) on abortion

    a. does not protect fetal life in the first trimester of life

    b. permits states to make laws to protect the fetus in the last trimester

    c. permits states to pass laws for the mother's health in the second trimester (but not the fetus')

    d. all of the above

    e. none of the above

Questions 4-7:

An 18-year-old young man and a 17-year-old young woman who have known each other for six months are contemplating "living together." In light of the STOP sign, list eight guidelines to help them form their sexual morality.

4. a.

   b.

5. a.

   b.

6. a.

   b.

7. a.

   b.

Questions 8-11:

The STOP sign. Fill in the requested information.

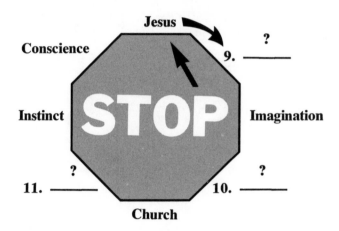

8. *Think?* What are the two elements in the T?

    a. ───────────────────────

    b. ───────────────────────

9. ───────────────────────

10. ───────────────────────

11. ───────────────────────

12. ───── If someone has never been taught that something he/
    she proposes to do is wrong, he/she must:

    a. follow his/her conscience
    b. be open to new data
    c. consult someone
    d. all of the above
    e. none of the above

13. ——— People ought to

    a. trust their "gut reaction" to moral situations because God is present to us

    b. distrust their feelings because feelings can be wrong

    c. both of these

14. List the Ten Commandments:

    a.   f.

    b.   g.

    c.   h.

    d.   i.

    e.   j.

15. ——— Which principle of good law does the following rule violate? (Assume that the law is made by a city government.) — "No one may eat ice cream on city streets."

    a. Law is reasonable.

    b. Law is for the common good.

    c. Law must be made by competent authority.

    d. Law must be promulgated.

    e. Not knowing the reason for the law, at face value this does not violate any principle.

16. ——— Which of the following statements does not represent Catholic morality?

    a. Be who you are.

    b. To be moral is to be human.

    c. In morality, all you need is love.

    d. The end does not justify the means.

    e. Do good and avoid evil.

Questions 17-19:

Consider this moral principle: If any element in a moral case is evil, the action itself should be considered wrong. In each pair of cases, identify what element is wrong (that is, the moral object, the intention or the circumstances).

17. ——————————— artificial contraception
    ——————————— driving while high on liquor
18. ——————————— joining a segregated golf club
    ——————————— profaning God's name
19. ——————————— murder
    ——————————— doing daredevil stunts on a bicycle
    in front of children

20. True or False. In most moral cases, there is usually only one or two alternatives to the proposed action.

21. ——— If a person is contemplating artificial insemination and is following the STOP sign model of moral decision-making, he/she ought to ask the following question first:

    a. Who is involved?
    b. What is artificial insemination?
    c. What are the consequences?
    d. Are there alternatives involved?
    e. When will it take place?

22. ——— An absolute determinist

    a. is Karl Marx
    b. would deny the reality of sin
    c. claims humans are not really free
    d. a and b
    e. a, b and c

23. In a couple of sentences, explain how morality is responsibility.

24. True or False. For Kohlberg, most people do their moral reasoning at the preconventional level.

25. ———— As defined in this book, which of the following is not
a characteristic of morality?

    a. a science
    b. concerned with the unreal
    c. guided by revelation
    d. concerned with human conduct
    e. assumes freedom

26. True or False. Catholic morality is significantly different from
Christian morality.

27. True or False. The Sermon on the Mount and the Beatitudes
are to the New Testament what the Ten Commandments are to the Old Testament.

28. The three elements of every moral action are (1) the moral
object; (2) the circumstances; and (3) ————————.

29. ———— The ethical teaching of Jesus

    a. is systematically presented in the New Testament
    b. has little relevance for us today
    c. hinges on the love of God and neighbor
    d. a and c
    e. none of the above

30. ———— If a person commits suicide, which principle of his/
her humanity is violated?

    a. We are social beings with and for others.
    b. We are historical beings.
    c. We have freedom.
    d. We are body-people.
    e. all of the above

31. List two Beatitudes and in a few words discuss the value preserved in the particular Beatitude.

    a.

    b.

32. The two principles involved in conscience are:

    a. You must follow your conscience.

    b. ———————————————.

33. ——— Which of the following represents a factual statement?

    a. A fetus is not human.

    b. Abortion is a form of contraception.

    c. The zygote has a programmed genetic package of a
human being.

    d. Because abortion is legal it is moral.

    e. none of the above

34. ——— Biblical images of sin include which of the following?

    a. a psychological disorder

    b. missing the mark

    c. hardness of heart

    d. mistake of judgment

    e. a and d

    f. b and c

35. ——— Which of the following did Pope Paul VI not advocate in his encyclical *Populorum Progressio?*

    a. 20 percent tax on the rich nations GNP (gross
national product)

    b. rectification of trade relationships

    c. creation of a world bank

    d. support of an international government

    e. more individual charity

36. True or False. In respecting human life, Catholics are obligated to do everything medically possible to
keep a person alive.

Questions 37-39:

What three conditions are necessary for a person to sin mortally?

37.

38.

39.

40. True or False. An accurate picture of sin pictures God as a
stern judge who is interested in justice.

41. ———— Which statement does not represent a Catholic position on right to life?

   a. Catholics have a right to work for a pro-life amend-
      ment.
   b. Human life begins at conception.
   c. Abortion is not a form of mercy-killing.
   d. A woman has an absolute right to her own body.
   e. In any situation, a Catholic may never will the
      abortion of a baby.

42. ———— "I want to abort because I am concerned about the
population problem." The person who thinks this
way is probably

   a. a utilitarian
   b. an extreme individualist
   c. a hedonist
   d. a Christian
   e. a rationalist

43. True or False. Conscience not only puts us in touch with who
we are but helps us decide the right thing to
do.

44. ——— Conscience is a(n)

    a. judgment
    b. feeling
    c. inner voice box
    d. none of the above

45. ——— When Jesus said that no one has any greater love than being willing to die for another, which of the following values did he give priority to?

    a. death
    b. life
    c. love
    d. property
    e. b and c

46. ——— Check the characteristics of a personal value from the following list.

    a. ——— one acts on it
    b. ——— it is prized
    c. ——— it is usually imposed
    d. ——— it is chosen without any alternatives in competition with it
    e. ——— consequences are considered

47. True or False. The church has a duty to teach in the area of morality.

48. ——— "All Catholics should attend Mass on Sundays."

    a. is a natural law
    b. is a church law binding on Catholics
    c. is a civil law for the functioning of church life
    d. as stated, is one of the Ten Commandments
    e. none of these

49. True or False.   Unlike human reason, imagination has little role to play in the solving of moral problems.

50. ———— Which of the following is not a characteristic of human life according to divine revelation?

    a. Being fundamentally evil, we have a fallen nature.
    b. We are words of God.
    c. We are children of God.
    d. We have the responsibility to care for nature.
    e. a and d

51. ———— "To give and not to count the cost" is

    a. narcissistic love   c. eros love
    b. agape love   d. philia love

52. Jesus most identified the love of God with the love of ————.

53. In a couple of sentences, explain why a Christian maintains that prayer is an important factor in making moral decisions.

54. ———— A person who says, "It is OK as long as I don't hurt anyone"

    a. might be ignoring unforeseen consequences
    b. fails to see clearly that everything one does affects others
    c. has a negative rather than positive image of morality
    d. all of the above
    e. none of the above

55. Which of the following questions reveal the circumstances of an action?

    ——— a. who   ——— d. when
    ——— b. what   ——— e. why
    ——— c. where   ——— f. how

56. ———— Which principle of Catholic morality holds that cheating on an exam in order to pass a test is wrong?

    a. The end does not justify the means.
    b. principle of double effect
    c. principle of proportionate good
    d. No circumstances can ever justify cheating.
    e. none of these

57. ———— If someone judged the rightness and wrongness of an action on consequences alone, he/she would tend to say:

    a. The greatest good for the greatest number of people.
    b. What moral principles are involved here?
    c. How will this benefit the individual?
    d. a and c
    e. b and c

58. ———— Teleological ethics is

    a. the ethics of Jesus
    b. mostly concerned with rules and regulations
    c. concerned with the consequences of an act
    d. a conformist morality
    e. all of the above

59. ———— A person who is not concerned with any standards of right behavior at all is:

    a. amoral   c. immoral

    b. moral   d. none of these

60. Our best guide to moral behavior is ————————.

SUMMARY

1. Milgram's research shows that the majority of people tend to conform to superior authority regardless of circumstances or consequences.

2. People conform to be accepted, to see themselves as correct, to be part of the group, to keep the group together and to achieve group goals.

3. Kohlberg's research shows that preconventional moral reasoning judges the rightness or wrongness of an act to avoid punishment (Stage 1) or for personal gain (Stage 2).

4. Conventional morality is characterized by a need for approval (Stage 3) or for upholding the law (Stage 4) for the sake of society.

5. Postconventional morality is manifested when a person sees that law is necessarily arbitrary and part of the social contract (Stage 5) or when a person acts out of principles of justice, the equality of humans and the respect for the dignity of others (Stage 6).

ANSWERS TO QUIZ

1. d; p. 202.
2. b; pp. 169-170.
3. d; p. 149.
4-7. A number of possible answers. See Chaper 5.
8. What are the alternatives? What are the consequences? pp. 41-43.
9. Reason and revelation; p. 13.
10. Law; p. 13.

11. Values; p. 13.
12. d; pp. 168-169.
13. c; pp. 102-104.
14. See pages 82-84.
15. e; pp. 79-80.
16. c; pp. 31-34.
17. object; circumstances; p. 39.
18. intention; object; p. 39.
19. object; circumstances; p. 39.
20. false; p. 40.

21. b; p. 29.
22. e; p. 18.
23. A response to God's love; an ability given at Baptism (the Spirit who prompts us to say "yes" to love), p. 22.
24. false; p. 220.
25. b; pp. 18-23.
26. false; pp. 23-24.
27. true; p. 81.
28. intention (motive); p. 39.
29. c; p. 59.
30. e; pp. 66-72.

31. See p. 84.
32. You must continuously inform your conscience; p. 105.
33. c; pp. 149-150.
34. f; p. 162.
35. a; p. 210.
36. false; pp. 191-193.
37-39. serious matter; full knowledge; consent of the will; pp. 168-169.
40. false; pp. 167-169.

41. d; pp. 142-143.
42. a; pp. 140-141.
43. true; pp. 105-107.
44. a; p. 105.
45. c; pp. 59-62.
46. a, b and e; p. 95.
47. true; p. 90.
48. b; p. 93.
49. false; pp. 74-77.
50. a; p. 72.

51. b; p. 59.
52. neighbor; p. 60.
53. It puts us in contact with Jesus who is both our guide and model in following the Father's will; pp. 50-53.
54. d; pp. 44-45.
55. a, c, d, f; p. 39.
56. a; p. 37.
57. d; p. 12.
58. c; p. 12.
59. a; p. 23.
60. Jesus; p. 59.